The

# E HIBITIONIST

To Judith,

Thanks for all your support!

Happy Reading!

Love from

Nichole

Steve

# *The* E**X**HIBITIONIST

## INSPIRING TRADE SHOW EXCELLENCE

### BY
### NICHOLA REEDER & STEVE REEDER

First published in Great Britain by
Practical Inspiration Publishing, 2019

ISBN 978-1-7886-0092-7

 Practical Inspiration
PUBLISHING

# CONTENTS

# ABOUT THE AUTHORS

Before you start on the journey to your trade show success, it might help to know a little more about us and why we're hoping to inspire you to think differently about your own campaign. In different ways we've been involved in trade shows and exhibitions for more than 20 years collectively, as exhibitors, visitors and helping organisers to add value to their events.

We started out much the same way as many of you will, inheriting the planning and execution of a trade show as a 'development' project, with a reasonably sized budget but very limited information on what had and hadn't worked in the past. The only way we learnt how to do it was to ask questions, lots of them, about everything from where to store huge boxes of chocolate or crates of beer, to which colours are most likely to catch a visitor's eye on graphics and how many staff to have on your stand. We asked everyone from event organisers to stand design agencies, visitors, other exhibitors, venue managers and logistics experts and found that everyone had a different version of the truth. One of the most important things we learnt on our own trade show journey is that there isn't one single truth when it comes to trade show execution. So much depends on the specific circumstances, objectives and resources of an organisation that not every piece of advice is going to work for every single exhibitor or event. However, there are some general principles that help provide a framework of best practice that help inform decision-making and generate powerful results.

## Steve Reeder

Logistics guru and lover of a planning spreadsheet, I thrive on working out how to get all your kit, equipment and people there on time, in full and with all the right permissions. My areas of expertise are in the operational aspects of trade shows, understanding the Exhibitor Manual and scheduling what needs to happen when to make sure an exhibition stand looks as engaging and professional as possible. As a quick-thinking problem-solver, I have overcome several challenges on behalf of clients including regularly finding homes for stock and kit when no one has booked storage, writing risk assessments and health and safety statements when exhibitors arrive on-site without either, and getting very large boxes through very small holes.

## Nichola Reeder

I thrive on discovering an exhibitor's commercial selling story and bringing that to life through their stand, pre-show marketing, squad training and follow-up. Finding the reasons why an exhibitor's product or service meets (and exceeds) a visitor's need brings the whole campaign to life, and for me it's the core to so many other decisions and actions that will ensure a trade show fills an organisation's sales pipeline. Having delivered trade show campaigns on behalf of multinational organisations, I also understand the crucial role the stand squad play in the success of the show and have trained exhibitors on how to engage, develop and filter visitors to ensure that the most valuable visitors become future buyers.

We've worked on several different projects as exhibitors ourselves as well as with clients who need either a guiding hand with their decision-making or want us to do all the work for them. We also work with event organisers on several exhibition elements including exhibitor training courses, developing and managing live theatre areas, visitor recruitment campaigns and working with high value sponsors and exhibitors to maximise their returns. Over the years we've heard the frustrations of so many exhibitors who feel they have wasted their money, or blame event organisers for poor results, yet we've seen so many fantastic executions that have generated solid commercial returns for businesses. Through *The Exhibitionist* we want to bring together some of the answers to the questions we've asked over the years and to provide some inspiration and food for thought that helps exhibitors, event managers and anyone involved in the industry to add more value to their campaigns and generate more profitable results.

# INTRODUCTION

*I'm in a hole because at some point I found a shovel
and started digging. Maybe I should trade my shovel for
ladders and start climbing.*

—Craig D. Lounsbrough, M.Div., LPC

Have you ever invested a significant amount of budget in a trade show, spent three days on your feet and not spoken to anyone of interest before thinking there must be a better way? Maybe you keep doing what you've always done because your company accepts it's 'just the way it is with trade shows'? Or maybe you're a business owner who really wants to get out and speak to your customers but is secretly terrified?

Congratulations! Just by picking up a copy of this book you're already on the first rung of the proverbial ladder to generating more profitable leads and better returns from your trade show investment. You're probably wondering how that's possible when you haven't even read a page yet? In our combined experience of 20 years' working on trade shows and events we'd say success is about 70% attitude, enthusiasm and a desire to learn and 30% what you actually do. Despite the digital evolution, face-to-face events remain a crucial element of the marketing mix with 99% of marketers from overperforming organisations believing that events provide visitors with a valuable opportunity to form in-person connections in an increasingly digital world (Bizzabo, 2018). But trade shows are often hard work – emotionally, physically and mentally. Not everyone has the necessary desire or disposition to deliver them brilliantly and that's not something any book can help with! Coupled with the perception that trade shows never deliver a measurable return, they are often easy targets for criticism and budget cuts from senior teams wowed by the latest social media platform. However just by picking up this book you've demonstrated the mindset for learning some new skills and taking some inspiration that will enable all your future trade show campaigns to act as the engine for your organisation's sales pipeline.

Often when we meet with clients for the first time there's a range of causes driving their trade show anxiety, from a lack of confidence and skill, to a lack of time and resource. They're always surprised when we tell them that they're not alone and that so many fellow exhibitors feel those same fears. There seems to be a culture in the industry that 'everyone can do trade shows', as though it's as easy as jumping out of bed in the morning. To a certain degree, it is easy to book last minute, turn up with a couple of mis-shaped pop-up banners, spend the day chatting with fellow exhibitors or on your laptop and then moan about the lack of business generated. However, to plan, implement and evaluate a trade show brilliantly, that engages with visitors and adds real value to your business through building profitable relationships for the future – now that takes skill, experience and dedication. But by picking up this book, we know you'll rise to the challenge!

There are so many sectors, variables, life stages, structures and budgets in business that it would be impossible to provide one blueprint for brilliant execution – one size most definitely does not fit all in this case. Equally, there aren't very many straight yes and no answers either, it's all about how a trade show fits in to your story and meets your customer's needs. However, in the following chapters we hope you find an easy-to-follow framework that walks you through the key elements of delivering a brilliant trade show campaign, from the initial enquiry about which show to attend, to calculating a final number of what your investment returned (yes that's possible, don't believe the hype about trade shows being unmeasurable). We'll be sharing some of the knowledge, tips, advice and examples we've collected over the years (good and bad) to help inspire your own trade show journey. If you're a seasoned exhibitor you may perceive some of the advice as simplistic or patronising but often when we're running workshops it's the simple things that people already know they want reminding of – we're trying to provide something for everyone so if there are bits you know, skip ahead to a bit that's new for you! Every trade show is different, as is every exhibitor and you'll need to give some thought to the content of each section on your own business circumstances. But there are plenty of ideas to help you understand how you convert your trade show investment into a winning proposition.

We've used some icons along the way that should help you steer your way around the content:

 Where you see this symbol there's a key piece of operational advice or a real-life example that will help you execute a better event. These are some of the basics you need to get right and these points should give you the core inspiration that you build everything else around.

 Where you see this symbol we're sharing a piece of industry insight or research to help illustrate why the suggestions we're making are important. Your internal stakeholders can be your toughest critics so hopefully by sharing some of the best evidence in the business you've got the ammunition you need to fight for the resources you need.

Where you see this symbol, we're sharing some inspirational or thought-provoking quotes with you to help inspire you along your journey.

## How to get the best of this book?

Ideally, we'd suggest reading the book in its entirety before starting on your planning to help you best understand how all the elements fit together as a jigsaw. We've broken it up into bite-sized chunks that should allow you to tackle and digest each building block as we navigate the whole process. In Part 1 we'll look at why trade shows are still relevant in the digital age and deciding whether trade shows are even the right tactic for your business in its current position.

The bulk of the book comes in Part II, which we've broken up into three further sections – Planning, Implementation and Evaluation (P.I.E.) where we will delve into the intricate details of executing your trade show campaign brilliantly; we have broken these down into sections, listed in the table of contents, to help you navigate through them easily. As mentioned, it's worth reading all three sections in their entirety before starting your journey, as there will be things you'll need to be thinking about in the planning stage to measure the right things for your evaluation! However, we know that might not be feasible so if you're pushed for time, we've made the contents table as simple as possible, so you can jump in and out of the specific areas where you feel you need the most help. In the Planning section we'll pick up on elements including researching the right show, budgeting, logistics, stand design and pre-show marketing to ensure that you're in the best possible shape to engage effectively with visitors. Moving into Implementation we look at the different roles required on a stand, typical characteristics of your squad and how to manage them as well as how to open conversations, filter visitors and identify the ones who have high potential for your business. After the show we look at Evaluation which includes how to follow up effectively (almost 90% of exhibitors don't) and how to calculate success including how to measure the business your investment has returned.

Finally, in Part III, as you build your confidence and skill, we go beyond the trade show floor and discuss exhibiting internationally and using the media to promote your message to really drive the value of your investment even harder.

There's a lot packed into this book and to do everything we're suggesting would be unrealistic (but if you do manage it, you're our hero!). We've concluded every chapter with a checklist of the key questions that should help you reflect on how you can use the advice to make the most effective decisions for your organisation. There will be things you're already doing really well (great, keep doing them), things that won't be appropriate for you and things we haven't included (even 20 years in, we're still learning every day). But even if you just select one or two tips and change your plans accordingly, we're pretty sure you'll see a positive effect on your outcomes.

If you've already got a trade show in mind and want to get maximum value from this book we'd recommend using it alongside **The Exhibitionist Project Manager Journal** (available from **www.inspiringexhibitors.com**) which will give you the tools, templates and timelines all in one handy folder that will help you track your progress and developments as you plan a fantastic event.

There will be regular blogs on the **www.inspiringexhibitors. com** website which will give you any new ideas that we've come across in the trade as well as fortnightly podcasts with experts from within the industry to help give you even more inspiration and advice. You can sign up for the Inspiring

Exhibitors newsletter via the website too. We'd love to hear your feedback about the book, your planning, what you've learnt and what more you need to know so please get in touch any time via Twitter (**@ProExTraCo**) or email **proextra@12th-man-solutions.co.uk**.

Trade shows and exhibitions are always evolving, and this book is just part of a much bigger conversation. The basic framework for delivering a great show hasn't changed much over the years, but the tactical execution, such as stand design and digital and social media are changing fast. The key factor in ensuring your tradeshows deliver meaningful and measurable results, is continuously building your company's exhibiting capability. How best to exhibit at trade events has been debated for decades and has become more complex, with the body of knowledge on executing profitable trade shows exploding. However, it's often hidden in pockets of excellence that in isolation don't give a full appreciation of the end-to-end process. Far too few exhibitors are keeping up with the changes and seeking out the latest thinking and best exhibiting practices. Many companies are operating on an exhibiting model that is 10 years out of date where they all seem to know what they are spending, but too few know what they are really getting in return or how to better it. By reading this book and acting on its contents you will undoubtedly improve the chances of generating more profitable leads from your investment and maybe you'll put your shovels away too and climb above your competitors! We wish you the very best of luck on your trade show journey.

*The beginning is the most important part of the work.*
—Plato, The Republic

# PART I

# WHY ENGAGE?

# CHAPTER 1

# WHY TRADE SHOWS MATTER EVEN MORE IN THE DIGITAL AGE

*It's hard to say exactly what it is about face-to-face contact that makes deals happen, but whatever it is, it hasn't yet been duplicated by technology.*

—Paul Graham, computer scientist, entrepreneur, venture capitalist, author and essayist

## The digitally connected world

From a worldwide population of over 7.5bn in 2017, there are 3bn active social media accounts, with people spending on average 2.5 hours a day scrolling through Facebook, Twitter, LinkedIn, Instagram and every other existing and emerging platform. That's 2bn active Facebook users, 500m of us on LinkedIn and over 1.3bn Twitter accounts plus Instagram, Pinterest, YouTube and all the others. In addition to all this frenetic social media activity, it's estimated over 269bn emails are sent globally every day with the average office worker receiving over 121 emails a day (Tschabitscher, 2018). The culmination of all this activity resulted in a staggering 2.3 trillion dollars of global on-line consumer spending in 2017 with predictions that this will grow to over 4.4 trillion dollars by 2021 (Statista, 2017). Therefore, you'd be forgiven for assuming that the internet was the holy grail for generating sales growth in our digitally engaged era, but the numbers only tell half a story. Dig a little deeper and all is not quite as promising as it first seems. Ninety-six per cent of people who discuss brands online don't follow the brand itself suggesting that although they are being 'talked' about there isn't necessarily a deep or sustainable relationship (Hainla, 2018). There are an estimated 270m fake Facebook accounts and of the 1.3bn Twitter accounts, only 300m are live, with only 1/3 of those being accessed daily. Whilst LinkedIn markets itself as a network for building business relationships, the average CEO has almost 1,000 connections (Sikandar, 2018), implying that whilst broad, the connections are unlikely to be deep or trusting. And remember those 269bn emails that get sent every day – almost 50% are registered as spam and never even make it to their intended recipient (Sikandar, 2018).

As a brand or service fighting to make itself heard in a crowded digital marketplace, the competition is tough with 65m business pages on Facebook, 500m daily Tweets, 300m company pages on LinkedIn (Sikandar, 2018) – not to mention the 95m images which are uploaded to Instagram every day and the 75bn ideas currently listed on Pinterest (Aslam, 2018). Admittedly, there are tools, software and agencies that can help ensure marketing content is generated and targeted so it hits the most relevant audience but that can suck up time, money and resource for any business regardless of size.

## Digital revolt

In addition to the mass of noise on social media, there is a growing tide of disengagement, with suggestions that our love of (un)sociable media may be reaching a tipping point. Growing reports of fake news, tampering with political elections, invasive advertising, jealousy over aspirational lifestyles, invasion of privacy, trolling and cyber bullying are leading us to question whether as a population we're starting to crave more human, emotional and meaningful relationships. Research from software provider Kapersky found that almost half of all respondents felt jealous when their friends' posts received more likes than their own (Ismail, 2017). Unsurprisingly 72% of people were frustrated with invasive advertising that interrupted their communications or distracted them from a transaction they were looking to complete (Ismail, 2017). Millennials particularly seem to be deserting the social media channels they have grown up with, seeking instead more immersive brand experiences which they can feel a part of. According to Origin, a Boston-based market research group, 34% of Gen Z'ers are saying goodbye to social media while 64% have decided to take a break from it (McAteer, 2018).

This trend is flowing through into brand planning, evidenced by the significant growth in experiential marketing budgets in recent years with organisations instead looking to invest in real-life experiences to build relationships and drive loyalty. Experiential marketing covers a broad range of different tactics but could include consumer roadshows, sponsorship, trade exhibitions, pop-ups, permanent installations and even augmented reality. *Campaign* research reported that in 2017 Chief Marketing Officers expected to allocate between 25–50% of marketing budgets to experiential tactics over the next 2–5 years. The research showed that positive results were being generated from deeper interactions with customers in both the Business-to-Business (B2B), selling through a third party and Business-to-Consumer (B2C), selling directly to the end user, environments with almost 60% agreeing that live events create the opportunity for deeper and more sustainable relationships which drive more frequent and higher value transactions.

## Case Studies of High Impact Experiential Campaigns 2017

1. **Organisation**: *David Lloyd — 'Run For Your Bun' Café*

   **Objective**: To demonstrate how healthy food and exercise form part of a balanced lifestyle

   **Execution**: Located in London, this pop-up witnessed customers ordering their healthy and nutritious lunch, following which they had to participate in a vigorous 10-minute workout before they were given their food. The activity targeted office workers to show how they could incorporate exercise into their day.

2. **Organisation**: *Adidas – 'D Rose Jump Store'*

   **Objective**: To introduce a new line in basketball footwear to the UK

   **Execution**: Pop-up stores aren't a new concept, but Adidas' 'D Rose Jump Store' in London was a cut above the rest. Chicago Bulls point guard Derrick Rose was in attendance to challenge fans to win a pair of free trainers by taking them off a shelf that happened to be 10 feet in the air. It was a relevant, exciting and memorable experience for all the children and parents who took part.

## Trade show traction

The B2B trade show and exhibition industry is certainly benefitting from the growing interest in experiential with over 31,000 certified events globally each year (UFI, 2014). Outside of the official events recorded with industry researchers, there are countless other smaller, regional and local roadshows, expos and networking events where suppliers and customers can discuss opportunities for working together. In one of their sourced blogs Eventbrite, the world's largest event booking provider, suggests that in the UK alone, the exhibitions sector contributes over £193bn to the economy through attracting global visitors and exhibitors as well as supporting UK based suppliers. They go on to explain that over 1.3m business events were held in the UK in 2017 with an estimated £40bn being spent in the local economy (Eventbrite, 2018).

Almost 4.5m companies exhibit globally at trade shows every year, welcoming over 260m visitors to their stands demonstrating the scale and power of live events (UFI, 2014). There are a number of reasons why an organisation will choose to exhibit at an event including generating new leads, launching a new product or service, building relationships with existing customers or to be part of an industry conversation (see Section 3.1, SMART objective setting). Regardless of the objectives a company sets for the specific event, the ultimate aim is to grow sales and profits and trade shows are increasingly being seen as a high potential platform through which to do it.

Ninety-one per cent of visitors state that attending a trade show impacts on their buying decision in some way (GraphiColor Exhibits, 2017), be that positively or negatively. From a well-planned and executed exhibition stand, a visitor takes away the perception of quality, reliability, value and trust. From a poorly planned exhibitor, the visitor leaves disappointed and anxious about how difficult any future relationship might be. Yet for those who do not even exhibit, a visitor could be impressed by the investment, quality and offer delivered by their competitor and choose to do business with them instead. It is worth noting at this point that we talk about a visitor 'doing business' in the future as trade shows of today facilitate making a connection for future business, rather than generating high value sales at the show itself. The roots of trade shows can be traced back to the medieval era when producers and craftsmen would travel between towns to showcase and sell their wares either to individual customers or to guilds on behalf of the town. The industrial revolution witnessed the evolution of trade shows into industry specific events focussed on selling products to a target group of commercial entities. Throughout the twentieth century events became a trading floor for deep-cut discounting and 'deal-led' activity where the cost of the show was minimal compared to the loss of profit on eye-watering deals. Increasingly trade shows have become a forum for bringing together those with a common interest to satisfy a conscious need and establish how they may work together in future. There are still some events which are highly transaction led but if this is not aligned to your specific objectives, some quick research should eliminate these shows from your radar (see Section 3.2, Which show?).

Trade shows facilitate a deeper conversation with a prospect than could ever be achieved in a 240-character tweet or Facebook post. Trade shows open up a conversation based on the buyer need, to understand how your product or service can help save them time or money, generate more profit or simplify their processes. Equally, it can also establish very quickly where your product or service isn't able to help meet the needs of the visitor and enable both parties to respectfully move on to more lucrative opportunities. Forty-seven per cent of marketers believe events are a highly efficient and effective way to reach and engage with multiple customers and prospects (Marketing Charts, 2013). The key qualifier here is being able to identify 'higher quality' prospects and leads, as having taken the time to understand the key problem a prospect is facing and how your product solves it, the follow up conversation becomes more effective and targeted.

*Studies by the Centre for Exhibition Research (CEIR) and Exhibit Surveys, Inc. show that closing a lead generated at a trade show costs almost forty percent less than a lead generated from the field.*
*(CompuSystems, 2010)*

A polite referral, or a review of a lead database, don't start to explore at a deeper level how a product meets a need, or whether two organisations can, and more importantly want, to work together. Trade shows and exhibitions bring together interested buyers and sellers who can collaboratively solve problems for mutual growth. Whilst social media and digital marketing tactics can deliver scale this often lacks depth, reaching only a tiny minority who may be in a position to buy. Whilst scale may benefit in driving brand awareness, without the depth of a conversation there is minimal opportunity for a buyer to understand whether a product or service can meet their needs.

Trade shows and exhibitions, although relatively expensive compared to social media activity, can be more efficient in bringing large numbers of an interested audience under one roof for a period of time. In just a few hours, organisations can engage with hundreds, if not thousands, of self-selected potential buyers that would take them months, if not years, to visit in the field. One area which we should emphasise at this point is that exhibitions are expensive, in time, money and emotion and they are not going to be the golden bullet which delivers 10,000 new customers the day after the show closes. To expect that would be unrealistic. This book is not intended to save you either time or money, in fact there are times we will encourage you to spend more. Exhibitions are expensive when you consider them in isolation and they take time, commitment and energy. Research from the USA suggests that companies are now investing up to 33% of their annual marketing budgets into trade shows (Levin, 2017) with respondents in a recent study stating that 47% of them plan to maintain budgets whilst 30% state that they are planning to increase theirs (Exhibitor, 2018). Budget will depend entirely on a number of variables but even if the average UK cost were £20,000 including all time, accommodation and travel expenses, stand fee, design and build etc. this looks expensive versus a couple of pounds to promote a Tweet or Facebook advert. However, the social media platforms cannot deliver the depth of relationships and the foundations of trust that can be built through an initial conversation with a visitor who has already declared an interest in your offer simply by attending the event.

## Measuring return – yes you can!

Whilst it is possible to share data relating to the value of the industry in terms of spend, it is much more difficult to evaluate the value of business generated from investing in trade shows. As social media and digital have become increasingly popular, a growing number of tools, systems and agencies have popped up to offer analytics and metrics to justify spend based on the number of clicks which subsequently convert to a sale. Why then, is it so difficult to measure for trade shows? The main reason is the lack of follow up from exhibitors with over 87% of leads collected at a show never being contacted by the exhibiting company (Davis, 2018). On average, 64% of stand visits at trade shows are from delegates who are not an existing customer of the exhibiting company but are interested in their product or service. Over half of all visitors go on to purchase from an exhibiting company within a year of meeting them at a trade show or event (Display Wizard, 2018) and an average of 51% of trade show attendees request that a sales representative visit their company after a show (Matthes, 2018). To reflect on those stats for a moment, only 13% of leads are followed up after a show, yet those exhibitors are doing business with just over half of all the visitors, therefore it is not difficult to image what the real value of trade could be if only all exhibitors followed up on their opportunities (see Chapter 5, Evaluation).  It is this lack of evaluation and an inability to determine a real return on investment that has seen trade shows lose popularity in recent years in favour of digital marketing tactics which are easier and more visible to measure.

*Ninety-five per cent of marketers agree that live events provide attendees with a valuable opportunity to form in-person connections in an increasingly digital world.*
*(Endless, 2018)*

Despite the lack of statistical evaluation on the return that trade shows deliver, there is a renewed interest in events, especially in light of the previous discussion regarding the need for deeper and more meaningful interactions with potential buyers. In a recent survey, over 91% of exhibitors stated that they believed trade shows and exhibitions would continue to be a critical element of their marketing strategy for the foreseeable future (Skyline, 2011). In addition to that, event organisers themselves are growing their own footprint with 88% of the US and European organisers stating they would be looking to add additional shows to their portfolios and expect visitor numbers to rise (UFI, 2018).

Therefore, would it be correct to assume that trade shows are the priority marketing tactic for organisations and brands should focus solely on investing in such events? Well, no, it's not quite that simple. As anyone involved in marketing will appreciate, an effective strategy depends on executing a range of tactics based on customer or consumer insight. Investing in trade shows or exhibitions is not a marketing strategy in its own right, as much as exhibiting at a show 'just because you always have' is not a strategic marketing tactic. The most effective investment in a trade show or exhibition will be made when it is supported by a range of other well thought-through and directed marketing tactics which appeal directly to solving the customer problem. We will discuss in future chapters the critical need to identify a customer problem and understand how your product or service helps resolve that, but once that is defined, several different methods could and should be employed to help close a sale. A trade show is just part of the on-going dialogue with a customer or consumer that establishes rapport and builds trust.

Although we have discussed a growing sense of unease and suspicion towards social media, research showed that social networks are now the most influential forum for both on and off-line purchasing (40%), ahead of the brand's own website or traditional media. Therefore, with a very broad audience and a relatively low cost of advertising it would be a brave organisation which chose to ignore the power of digital and social media altogether. In Chapter 3 we will talk about pre-show marketing in which we discuss how powerful social media and direct marketing can be in ensuring that the right visitors are coming to your stand when the show is open. This clearly demonstrates where on-line and off-line marketing techniques can work in parallel to achieve a stated objective.  Even where pre-show marketing reaches more broadly than your specific target audience, it is still part of the conversation in building brand awareness and articulating how you meet a need.

We very often have clients who will ask 'But why do I need to do a trade show when everyone just stares at a phone all day now?' – which is a fair question! If nothing else, a trade show will give you the opportunity to spend a couple of days actually engaging with humans and sharpening up your inter-personal skills!  Aside from that, social media and digital isn't enough on its own for very many companies, in the same way that just broadcast media, or PR or trade shows on their own wouldn't be enough. Powerful marketing comes from the ability to target and execute effective techniques that complement each other and build an on-going conversation with your customer.  It isn't a competition with marketing tactics battling each other for precedence (although we've sat in many budget planning sessions where it's felt like that). Trade shows give you relevant content to talk about on social media and social media gives you a wide platform to talk frequently about what you're doing at the show. It's all about being part of the same conversation!

*Today, people don't trust companies. One of the things marketers want to do is to humanise their brand. What better way to do it than put a live person in front of them?*

—Jackie Huba, dynamic keynote speaker, bestselling author and expert on customer loyalty and evangelism

## Summary

Although it may seem that digital and social media is taking over the world, there's a growing bank of evidence that would suggest as humans we're starting to look for deeper and more meaningful experiences, especially from those organisations we are considering buying from. Trade shows become powerful as a tactic alongside social media and digital to help engage with those existing and potential customers at a deeper level.

In summarising why trade shows are even more relevant in the age of digital and social media it's worth considering the following key points:

- Although there are over 3bn social media accounts globally, many are either fake or inactive with the remaining platforms generating significant noise and competition

- Increasingly the global population is becoming suspicious of social media and turning away from it in search of deeper and more meaningful engagements – this includes from brands and organisations

- 31,000 registered trade shows are held annually every year with over 4.5m exhibitors and 260m visitors proving that they are still highly popular and relevant as a customer relationship tactic

- Ninety-one per cent of visitors state that their buying decision is affected by what they see at trade shows – both positively and negatively

- The cost of converting a sales lead generated from a trade show can be almost half the cost of converting a lead generated from other sourced such as referral or lead databases

- Fifty-one per cent of visitors buy from an exhibitor that they have met within 12 months of the show

- Trade shows rarely work in isolation and the digital and social media tactics available today are of massive benefit in maximising success at a trade show as part of an aligned marketing strategy (the subject of our next chapter).

# CHAPTER 2

# ARE TRADE SHOWS THE RIGHT TACTIC FOR YOUR BUSINESS?

*All men can see these tactics whereby I conquer, but what none can see is the strategy out of which victory is evolved.*

—Sun Tzu, c. 6th century BCE Chinese general, military strategist and philosopher, *The Art of War*

In the previous chapter we provided you with some compelling evidence as to why trade shows remain a crucial part of the marketing mix even in this digitally engaged world Hopefully now you're feeling enthused, energised and ready to get started on planning your next trade show. However, before you dive in and start investing your hard-earned cash in branded giveaways and bespoke animations to play on your 100-inch plasma screen, there's another piece of the jigsaw you need to make fit – and that's to consider whether trade shows are even the right tactic for your brand and your business. You might find it strange that in a book that strongly advocates the role of trade shows and seeks to inspire exhibitors to deliver better events, we're even suggesting that trade shows might not be the best tactic. This comes from decades of working with a wide variety of brands and organisations that have spent tens of thousands on individual trade events that were never going to return much value. Before we get into the excitement and specifics of making your trade show brilliant, let's talk about whether it even has the potential to be brilliant to begin with.

## Where is your business now?

Before you invest in any trade show or event, or any marketing tactic in general, stop and ask yourself where your business is now and where it is going. If you're the owner of the business, where do you want to be in the next 3–5 years and who are the customers and stakeholders who will help you get there? If you're employed by an organisation, do you understand the corporate vision and mission and are you clear on where the business is looking to grow?

For example, imagine you're working in a business that develops a product or service that will exclusively be sold online to the end user without the need for an intermediary wholesaler or retailer. Your business is based on an e-commerce model where the consumer visits your website or app to buy your product or service and can receive additional content and information about you direct to their inbox. You are the only provider in the market for your niche product and your target audience, while incredibly loyal, are spread across the globe. Having recruited a consumer, usually by referral from within their online community, they are frequent and high-value buyers and you build a relationship by adding value to their experience with you. Your ambition is to grow your current sales by extending your portfolio of services.

In this set of circumstances, it would be difficult to justify the cost of investing in trade shows as a marketing tactic. Certainly, a B2B event would deliver little value as your route to market is directly to the consumer and therefore visitors who are attending an event on behalf of their business would not be relevant for your specific growth objectives. A B2C event *might* have more potential if it were in a complementary industry but the relative costs versus the limited number of possible customers you might meet would make it a very expensive and low-value investment. Building online advocacy and enhancing the user experience would be far more relevant in these circumstances than a trade show would be. Understanding who and where your audiences are is a critical first step in deciding whether trade shows will be the right tactic for your business. Before even thinking about which trade show to attend, what your stand looks like and who's going, ask yourself honestly if trade shows are a tactic that could reach an audience that can contribute to your growth aspirations?

### Case study: ASOS

1. **Organisation:** *ASOS – As Seen On Screen*

   **Objective:** To become the number one global online fashion destination for 20-somethings

   **Execution:** ASOS delivered revenues in 2017 of £1.9 billion, exclusively through an online platform of affordable, trendy and authentic clothing ranges, aimed at 20-somethings but purchased by a much wider age group. ASOS's success has been driven by significant investment in delivering a brilliant online user experience, supported by good customer service and seamless integration across desktop and mobile. Their audience grew up surrounded by digital and live their life on and through their devices. Although some advertising has been executed offline, with print and outdoor media, it is largely done online, where their audience spend most of their time. In these circumstances and with this objective it would be difficult to argue the merits of investing in trade shows with the possible exception of perhaps some consumer clothing and fashion events.

*Even despite this digital success, ASOS has been a victim of the consumer desire for a more in-depth and tactile relationship putting-out  a profits warning 17th Dec 2018 based on slowing sales growth.

## Are you ready to sell?

The key long-term objective of any trade show is to establish new relationships, or build on existing ones, in order to achieve profitable sales growth. But what if you don't have anything ready to sell? Many new businesses, or existing businesses with a new product, rush to exhibit at their industry trade show with a few mocked-up samples and a rough product cost but without any thought to a solid route to market strategy. One of the most common complaints we hear from visitors is that they have found an amazing new product at an event, but they can't actually buy it yet. Or they can only buy it direct from the manufacturer in either small or huge quantities which just aren't appropriate. When you're passionate about your product or service, and need it to start earning money for you, it's tempting to get lost in the excitement and forget about the practicalities of getting your product to your customer. However, if you disappoint a potential new customer during the first interactions you have with them, it is much more difficult to rebuild that trust when you are ready to sell. As we will keep coming back to throughout this book, trade shows are not about what's important to you or your business, but what's important to your customer – and if you can't make the transaction easy you might question whether you should wait.

This also raises the question of scalability. Trade shows attract a range of visitors with very different buying authority from different sized businesses. There is always the potential you might meet someone who wants to order more stock than you could ever produce based on your current capacity – how would you manage that conversation so that they work with you rather than taking your idea and asking a company with a larger capacity to manufacture it for them? Equally, if everyone you meet wants to place orders for immediate delivery would you be able to service the demand? We're not suggesting that you wait until every piece of the jigsaw is in place before you unleash your brilliance on the market, in business things are rarely ever perfectly finished. The point is to really think about whether you're ready enough to be exhibiting and whether you have good enough responses for the areas where you're not quite ready yet?

*The No. 1 reason for visiting (not exhibiting at) trade shows is to see new products. More than 90% of trade show visitors say they are looking for new products. It has been the No. 1 reason to attend for 25 years! Trade shows are a great place to introduce or feature your newest products.* (Lincoln West, 2016)

## Is your customer ready to buy?

You may have put in all the hard work to ensure that your product or service is market ready (or as close to market ready as possible), but do you know that your customers are ready to buy? If you're operating in an established category or industry, where your product is an enhanced version of something already available, there is less risk. You know your customer wants this product or service and as long as you can clearly articulate why your proposition is better (faster, cheaper, easier, adds more value) than the competition, you have grounds for a credible commercial conversation.

However, if you're looking to build an entirely new category or industry with your product or service can you articulate why this is currently missing in their life? In these situations, customers and consumers might not even realise that they have a need for your product, meaning you will have to educate them about both the need and why yours is the best solution. A crowded trade show environment, with lots of distractions and minimal space to articulate your message might not be the most conducive place to start engaging with your audience.

Again, this comes back to grounding your trade show investment in customer need, understanding what their problem is and clearly articulating how your product or service provides the best solution for it. Therefore, in considering whether trade shows might be the best tactic for your business, it is helpful to think about the likely problem a visitor is going to be bringing to your stand and whether you can clearly articulate the solution you offer.

 *Forty-six per cent of trade show visitors are in executive or upper management roles. That's a lot of valuable*

*attendees with top titles walking trade shows. They certainly have the authority to make buying decisions!*
(Lincoln West, 2016)

## What else do you have in your toolkit?

We talked in Chapter 1 about using trade shows as a marketing tactic in an aligned, strategic plan and it's important to think about this further when considering whether exhibiting is right for your business. There will be several different sales levers you are likely to manipulate in your quest for sales growth, including pricing, promotions, discount structures, product variations, volume bonuses, etc. Each of these need determining before you can effectively manage a wider portfolio of customers. For example, if you're a manufacturer of tools you may offer a different discount level to an independent high-street DIY store than you would to a national wholesaler such as Screwfix – but you might meet both at the same trade show. Understanding how you will profitably manage different customer requirements and needs within your portfolio will not only help you to better filter visitors at the trade show itself but enable a quicker and more productive follow-up after the show.

In clarifying your sales strategy, it is likely that some obvious marketing tactics fall out of this to reach your audience and add value to the conversation you have with them. Let's go back to the tool example for a moment, potentially this could be a complicated purchase for your end user in selecting the most appropriate tool for his specific job. In that case, providing factsheets with details about what types of job each tool is most appropriate for will help them make an informed decision and ensure they are happy with their purchase. Although that is an example of a consumer marketing tactic, it's important to your trade show plan in demonstrating to your customer how you will help them sell through the products that you're selling directly to them. Developing a clearly aligned marketing plan across all channels will add value to the conversations you have at trade shows and build credibility and trust with your customer. Trade shows are rarely an effective tactic if used in isolation, or because you have always exhibited at them, or just because they sound like a good idea. The power of trade shows comes from alignment with a range of other trade and consumer marketing tactics that support each other as part of a proactive and strategic plan.

## Can you afford it?

*Corporate events and tradeshows usually fly under the radar when times are good and then are scrutinized when times are bad. But it's clear that reducing exposure at events is risky to future sales, and that attendance has recovered solidly following the past two economic downturns.*

—Michael Hughes, MD, Research and Consulting, Access Intelligence

Trade shows are notoriously expensive – there's not really any other way of saying it. They're not easy, and to do them well takes time, money and energy. If you're not prepared or in a position to invest a lot of all three, then trade shows may not be the right tactic for your business. We will talk more about monetary budgets in Chapter 3, but if you're going to invest in a trade show then invest well – in time and money. So often we hear from companies who have invested thousands of pounds in space on a trade show floor, then don't want to spend any more money on a stand or marketing so turn up with a couple of pop-up banners and one person to man the stand. At the end of the show we hear such exhibitors complaining about the lack of traffic at their stand, the conversations they haven't had and why they're never attending the show again – before signing on the dotted line for next year for fear of missing out (FOMO).

It is true to say that trade shows are difficult to evaluate and quite often businesses can be reluctant to spend big on them for fear of a lack of transparency on return. It may be difficult to demonstrate a return, certainly an immediate one, but it is not impossible. The setting of specific, measurable, achievable, realistic, timely (SMART) objectives and a clear follow-up strategy are crucial to the process of calculating return on investment (ROI) and we'll help you understand how to do both throughout the book. But don't be afraid to spend money on trade shows – just be sure you're spending it well and squeezing every single opportunity out of the cash you're putting in. If, however, you've only got the budget to book your space and nothing more, we'd advise you to think twice about whether trade shows are the right tactic for you. There are clever ways to spend a small budget, there are no clever ways to spend no budget.

In terms of resource, exhibitors can often be quite surprised at how much time needs to go into delivering an effective exhibition. Planning for a trade show can never start too early and ideally would be at least 12 months out from the start of the show (don't panic if you've a show coming up in a couple of weeks and you've done nothing yet, this book can still help).

The time spent on executing a trade show well becomes more intensive as the show approaches and in the last few weeks can almost feel like a full-time job – but investing the time into getting the right people to your stand on the day gives you a much greater potential for demonstrating a return on your investment. If you're a single business owner trying to wear the hat of production manager, marketing manager, HR, finance and logistics that could understandably sound daunting! The trick is to get organised, plan early and be prepared for the amount of time it's going to take – or call in the experts to help ease the load!

## Are you excited?

*Without leaps of imagination or dreaming, we lose the excitement of possibilities. Dreaming after all is a form of planning.*

—Gloria Steinem, writer, lecturer, political activist and feminist organiser

If you're not excited yet (even if it's nervously excited), then we'd suggest closing this book and handing it all over to someone else who does get excited by trade shows and who can manage your exhibition ambitions for you. Quite often there's an assumption that everyone loves doing trade shows and everyone knows how to do them. That's simply not the case and for some people just hearing that statement can come as a relief. Trade shows are hard work, physically, mentally and emotionally both in the run-up to and during the show itself, and they're not for everyone. If you don't enjoy the process, if you're not buzzing on build day and enthusiastic about all the new contacts that you're planning to meet, then visitors will see it in how you and your stand are presented. It will look forced and contrived and visitors won't feel welcomed or comfortable engaging with you. If strategically trade shows are important to your business but you're not the right person to project manage it, you have options, either within your own team or through outsourcing to partners who can organise absolutely everything for you. As Richard Branson has said many times, one of the qualities of a great leader is surrounding yourself with people who are better than you at the things you can't do.

If you're nervously excited, that's great and something you should definitely embrace. The excitement will give you the motivation and energy to get you through and the nervousness will help you consider all the elements to make well-balanced decisions. One thing that might help at this stage is understanding what specifically is making you nervous. Is it the fact you will need to justify spend to your manager and you're not sure how? Have you got a very functional product or service and you're worried about how to create impact and attract attention? Is this your first time and you're worrying about everything? All of these are perfectly understandable concerns, but none are insurmountable with some planning, some time to think and a bit of friendly advice (all of which you can find between these pages).

## Summary

So, while this book is all about how fantastic trade shows can be in boosting your sales pipeline, we've been around long enough to know that for many businesses it's just not the right tactic or the right time to help them achieve their long-term goals. As enthusiastic as you may be about heading off to Las Vegas with your mega-stand in tow, if the team back at the ranch haven't yet nailed how they're going to actually make your product in any great quantity, you may just fall at the first hurdle. Here are a few things in summary from this chapter to help sense check that trade shows will work effectively for your organisation:

- Consider your organisation's objectives for the next 3–5 years and identify what role (if any) trade shows play in reaching the right audience to achieve those aims.

- Be honest about how ready your business is with the product/service you're looking to sell and the capacity at which you can produce it. You don't want to create more problems for yourself by over-promising to potential new customers.

- Review your customers' readiness to buy your product and consider what else you might to do to help them realise they have a problem to which your product/service is the answer.

- If you know you have some gaps in the finer details of your product launch but are keen to exhibit to build momentum, make sure you have refined the answers for all the tricky questions visitors might ask about when and how they can get their hands on it.

- Review your whole marketing plan in the context of how trade shows maximise the other tactics you're using and make sure you have alignment across the core objectives, messaging and actions. Trade shows rarely work in isolation and are most powerful when all the different levers work together to promote each other.

- Be honest about the amount of time, money and resource you'll need to execute a trade show brilliantly from the start and where you don't have enough of any consider how you can find more internally or get the external expertise you'll need.

- Listen to your gut – if you're not feeling butterflies, either from excitement or anxiety, think about passing the project management onto someone else. Trade shows are tough enough without feeling as though every decision, every form and every day on the show floor is a chore – it will show in every aspect you deliver if your heart's not really in it!

With this book still firmly in your grasp, even though it may be with some nervous tension, over the following three chapters your exhibition journey truly begins, and we are here for you all the way. As mentioned in the introduction, although we have presented it as Planning, Implementation and Evaluation, it's not a directly linear process and there are some elements in Evaluation that you'll need to consider as part of your Planning. So, our advice, if you can, is to get to the end of the book before you start on your journey and everything will make more sense!

*Follow your dreams, let them guide you. Who knows where they may take you.*

—Nico J. Genes, *Magnetic Reverie*

# PART II

# P.I.E.

# CHAPTER 3

# PLANNING

*Give me six hours to chop down a tree and I will spend the first four sharpening the axe.*

—Abraham Lincoln

If you've decided having read the first two chapters that trade shows have a strategic role to play in meeting your organisation's objectives, you're probably eager to just get on the trade show floor and start talking to all those great new contacts. Hang fire though, great results from trade shows don't happen by accident and the more you can put into the planning and preparation for your events, the more you are likely to get out. Just as Abraham Lincoln knew the most effective way of chopping his tree down was to invest the time to get his tools right, the more time you can dedicate to getting all your trade show tools in shape, the more likely you are to attract the right kind of visitors to your stand, and actually recognise them when they arrive.

## Why visitors visit

Before we get too deeply into, and too excited by, your own planning, we want to challenge you to flip your thinking into your customer's world for a moment – the more you can ground everything you do in solving your customer's problem, the more likely you are to have a meaningful conversation with them. Visitors aren't going to engage in a conversation with you because *you* like your product or service, or to do *you* a favour – they'll keep talking because you've listened and identified their needs and are showing how you can help solve them. However, here's the science bit that shows from research the reasons why visitors attend trade shows in priority order:

- Exposure to new products and services
- To get more information on a specific product or service
- To reinforce or confirm existing buying decision
- To buy something
- To keep up to date on industry trends and innovations
- To make more industry contacts

*Ninety-one per cent of attendees state that exhibitions impact on their buying decisions and product placement.* (GraphiColor Exhibits, 2017)

## When to start planning

It's never too early to start thinking about how you will exhibit at a show, even if you don't even have a trade show in mind yet. If you're a first-time exhibitor and wondering whether trade shows are the right strategy for you, take the time to imagine what your trade show stand might look like, the sorts of conversations you would want to have, the type of potential and existing customers you might want to meet there and the outcomes you would want to achieve. This initial thinking will help contribute to a clear, strategic plan for your event, that informs a number of decisions you will make as you move through the planning process. Keep that vision and those conversations in your mind, write them down to keep yourself grounded in the reasons why you're investing all the time and money that will be needed to deliver brilliantly. If you're a seasoned exhibitor and you're wanting to generate more effective results from your events, think about the previous events you've delivered. What worked, and didn't for you? Which elements do you recognise you're weaker in? The more you can pinpoint the reasons why your trade shows aren't working as hard for you as they could be, the better chance you have of being able to understand how you can execute them more effectively next time.

To put a more specific timescale on when to start planning, ideally give yourself 12 months ahead of the show dates to plan effectively. This might sound like a luxury, especially if you're a business owner with responsibility for every aspect of operations, or if your role as trade show project manager is just one element of a hybrid responsibility. The word we use here is 'ideally' and 12 months is a fantastic lead time if you have it. If you don't, whatever the length of time before your show, you can still plan and improve your outcomes. Even if it's only two weeks until your event, you can still take the ideas in this chapter and put them to good use to enable you to deliver a more impactful and effective show. In fact, we've run Exhibitor Bootcamps on the morning of a show opening and exhibitors have told us they still learnt something that changed what they did during the day that impacted positively on their results. In short, start as early as you possibly can but never think it's too late to start either.

## 3.1 SMART objective setting
We so often hear that exhibitors have no way of evaluating trade shows and therefore they can earn the perception of being a money pit with no measurable return on investment. It's certainly true that trade shows can be harder and longer-term to evaluate than the effectiveness of other tactics such

as pay-per-click via social media, discount promotions or television advertising. However, harder and longer-term does not mean impossible, it just means it requires more effective planning up-front to ensure that you're clear about what you are trying to measure.

> *On average, companies allocate about 32% of marketing budgets to events and their stands. However, 70% have no specific objective for attending those events!*
> (Levin, 2017)

However, let's stick up for trade shows for a moment, as they can become a very easy target for dismissal in comparison to more 'measurable' tactics such as those mentioned above. Quite often social media or email campaigns are measured on a return on an objective, such as number of re-tweets, opens, click-throughs or likes. Where an organisation does not have a direct e-commerce platform there is no way to judge how those metrics have converted to actual cash purchases. Equally, television or radio advertising can drive awareness and approximate numbers for how many viewers or listeners may see or hear an advert can be measured. However, again it is difficult to measure how many of the eventual purchases of a product have been influenced by the media that the consumer has digested. And be honest, how many of us just store TV programmes and fast forward through the adverts these days? Finally, in respect of promotional discounts, these may be the most transparent in judging the effectiveness of a marketing tactic by driving additional sales but without investing in deeper research around customer metrics, it is difficult to identify how many consumers were going to buy the product anyway, how many are cupboard-filling and won't buy for several months and how many are impulse purchases driven by the promotional activity. However, in all these instances it is easy to measure achievement of objective, for example:

*Brand A deploys a social media campaign to drive awareness of its new product. The overall campaign is intended to:*

a.  *drive interested buyers to the website to learn more about the product and*

b.  *convert this interest to a purchase in their local store.*

*The campaign will consist of:*

- *Sending a targeted email to 50,000 customers on its mailing list.*

- *Upweighting Tweets to five a day, increasing two-way conversations and investing in Twitter advertising.*

- *Starting an Instagram account, posting two images a day and running some sponsored content.*

- *Creating a weekly blog post about how its product is being used by consumers in unusual and interesting ways.*

*The social media campaign will run in parallel to consumer sampling activity, the retailer's own marketing activity and promotions and general PR.*

In this example, it would be straightforward to attach measurement metrics to the objectives such as number of opens of an email, click-throughs to the website from Twitter ads or views and shares of blog posts or Instagram. What would be much harder to calculate are the resulting sales of the new product based on the social media campaign on its own, as it isn't being run in isolation. As we have already discussed, trade shows shouldn't be run in isolation either but as part of a fully aligned marketing campaign. Therefore, what can be measured accurately and effectively is the cost of achieving objectives that contribute to an overall return on investment. Assumptions can be made on the number of consumers who subsequently go on to purchase a product and this can contribute to a deeper discussion about return on investment, but it will be based on a number of hypotheses based on possible consumer behaviour.

No doubt a number of highly skilled marketers will argue that there are very many platforms, software and expert resources available that can measure the effectiveness of campaign activity very accurately, which is a fair point. If you run no marketing activity at all and sell ten widgets a week at £10, then spend £100 on some activity that increases sales to 30 widgets a week, it doesn't take a rocket scientist to work out a return on investment – every £1 invested has earned an incremental £2. But will those buyers who bought it once buy it again in future? Is it reaching a new audience or people who bought it anyway? Why did it only increase sales to 30 and not 50? Much ROI analysis can tell you what happened in relation to a limited number of direct elements but fails to look deeper into the why or how and implications for the future. We're not here to argue the merits or otherwise of measuring different types of marketing activity, it's simply to say don't let someone fob you off with an argument that trade shows aren't worth investing in because you can't measure ROI when so many other marketing tactics get away with measuring objectives achieved and not actual ROI.

## How do you measure a trade show?

Phew, now we've got that out of the way – there's absolutely no excuse for not setting some SMART objectives for your trade show activity and there are most definitely ways you can measure whether your event has delivered what you set out to achieve. When we ask exhibitors, 'What's your objective for attending a trade show?', we so often get the response, 'To meet people', and that's about as much thought as goes into it. If that is genuinely your objective then undoubtedly, you'll achieve it, just through meeting security when you arrive, the bar man at the hotel, a bloke in the toilets who's at a different event in the same venue and the cleaner who tidies up your stand but can any of those people contribute to the delivery of your overall business objectives? Getting SMART about your objectives focuses your mind for every subsequent decision you make about how to spend money on a show and how that contributes to achieving your overall business strategy. But how do you get SMART in the context of trade shows?

Looking back to Chapter 2 remember why you decided that trade shows were even the right tactic for your business in the first place – what is it about a trade show that makes you confident it can contribute to the overall delivery of your plan?

Some of the big marketing ideas (macro objectives) for exhibiting at a trade show might be:

- Entering a newly identified market with an existing product or service

- Launching a new product or service into an existing market

- Entering a new market with a new product or service

- To drive brand awareness in a current market with existing and prospect customers

- To be part of the industry conversation
- To collaborate or initiate a conversation with partners who could be useful

These are not so great examples of objectives for exhibiting at a trade show but ones we have heard before:

- Because we always have
- Because the organiser is a mate of the boss
- Because it was cheap
- Because I fancied a trip to Spain/USA/Birmingham
- Because the competition exhibit there (that's a tough one – see below)

The first step in setting SMART objectives that actually mean something to your business plan is working out specifically why you're exhibiting and that should be fairly obvious from the thinking you did in Chapter 2. Picking up on exhibiting because 'the competition are', it is admittedly a tricky argument. There is some credence in the suggestion that if your competitors are exhibiting at a show it is likely to attract the same visitors who you could do business with and that provides you with an audience. It is equally worth noting that you may be conspicuous by your absence and as shows impact the buying decision of 91% of visitors (GraphiColor Exhibits, 2017), by not being there, the only decision a potential customer can make is to buy from someone else. However, exhibiting just because a competitor is doesn't make a strong enough objective on its own. What if your competitor is much bigger than you, with more money to invest, making you look inferior by comparison even though you know you have a better product? Is there a more creative and less comparable way you can engage with them to demonstrate your quality? What if your competitor is only exhibiting because they always have without thinking about whether it's right strategically for them – it's a bad reason for them to exhibit and a doubly bad reason for you just to copy. So there might be a good reason to exhibit if your competitors are, but you probably need to explore more deeply if there are other reasons why it's right for you. Also, remember the visitor's perception of a company and brand that isn't supporting an industry show can reduce by as much as 5% (Russo, 2017).

If you've figured out the big reason why you're going to invest thousands, potentially tens of thousands of pounds in a trade show, congratulations, but you're only halfway there in terms of SMART objectives and there's still a bit more work to do. Just knowing you want to launch in a new market doesn't tell you who you're going to meet, how many you want to meet or how you're going to communicate your expertise and start building those relationships that are eventually going to lead to profitable sales. So how do you set SMART objectives for what is considered such an intangible tactic? It might help to sit down at this point and imagine being back in the office the day after a show, talking to your colleagues who ask you 'So was it a success?'. Imagine having an answer ready for them that starts 'Yes, because...' while you're able to reel off all the great things that have happened and how they will specifically contribute to the delivery of your organisation's business plan.

So here are some ideas that might inspire you towards setting your own SMART objectives:

- To distribute 3,000 samples of our new product variety to visitors

- To host five demonstrations with 20 interested buyers at each session

- To contribute to a live panel discussion featuring two of the key thought leaders in the industry

- To make contact with five high potential prospects and secure a follow-up meeting

- To give out literature and contact details to 100 interested browsers

- To ensure 2,000 visitors leave with our giveaway that reminds them what we do

- To meet the senior team from our top five customers

These are just generic examples and there will be hundreds of other examples that are possible based on the industry you work in. We will talk more about definite buyers and interested browsers in Chapter 4, but not every visitor to a show will be a potential buyer of your product, however well you've done your research, so it's useful early on to manage expectations and understand what's realistic in terms of contact. However, if you do know the average order value for customers you can start to add some more specific figures about the number of contacts you're likely to meet, potential conversion rates and possible order values that start to bring your objectives to life, especially for a sales team who are always focused on the numbers.

Another comment we often hear in relation to setting objectives is 'we want to meet everyone who attends', which is an admirable if somewhat challenging aspiration. This is so often the default position for exhibitors who think that trade shows are all about meeting as many people as possible without considering the resource needed on the stand to talk to that many people, never mind the sales force required to follow up with them. In reality, research shows that on average 16–20% of a trade show audience will be able to buy your product or service (Bailey, 2004). Without any targeting or filtering, gathering contact details for every random visitor who attends the show becomes a value-less experience. Exhibitors fail to engage with visitors who have a real prospect of buying in the haste to move on to scanning the next person's business card. It's worth remembering that just one or two high-value contacts at a show could return more in orders than the cost of the show itself. We will go into how to engage and filter visitors in more detail in Chapter 4.

So, just to clarify, when setting SMART objectives, the key rules are:

- **Specific:** Who, what, how many?
- **Measurable:** Can you record it?
- **Achievable:** In the context of the resource you have available.
- **Realistic:** Be honest.
- **Timely:** Within the parameters of the event.

We're not suggesting setting objectives is easy, it isn't, especially with so many variables but it is massively helpful in informing all the difficult decisions you're about to make and in evaluating how successful you've been. And don't forget our earlier point about return on investment versus achieved objectives – we'll talk in Chapter 5 about evaluating ROI, return of objective (ROO) and cost of objective (COO) which can only happen 6–12 months after a show (unless you're lucky enough to be actually selling at an event). The benefit of setting these objectives is that it will give you an immediate review of how effective your tactics have been at the show long before any business has been done.

> *The top three sales-related objectives at trade shows are related to relationship management and engagement. Above all else, exhibitors want to meet with existing customers, key customers and prospective customers according to CEIR. (Thimmesch, 2013)*

## 3.2 Which show?

Were you baffled by the number of global exhibitions we mentioned in Chapter 1 – 31,000 globally certified every year (UFI, 2014)? And that's not counting all the smaller regional and business networking events you might get the opportunity to participate in. So how on earth do you decide which is the right show for you? Well, the good news is that if you've worked out what you want to achieve from investing in a trade show, the process of selecting one (or several) should be much easier and then it's just down to research, research, research! Think you don't have time to do the research? Isn't it better to spend 2–3 hours researching the right show rather than waste the time, money and energy involved in being at the wrong show for three days?

One point to clarify before we proceed is the terminology around trade shows and events, which can be confusing, even to exhibitors who have been working in the industry for years.

- **Exhibition:** Quite often confused with a public installation or museum collection, but in this context, an event with a number of organisations with similar interests, products or services in a central location, with the aim of attracting visitors who are interested in purchasing those products or services. May also include some elements of live theatre or knowledge exchange.

- **Trade show:** Can be used interchangeably with exhibition in this context, although little 'trading' is actually done in modern trade shows, with the emphasis being more on meeting contacts and establishing relationships.

- **Seminar:** Content-led events or elements of trade shows that focus on sharing expertise and adding value through educating and engaging with a visitor.

- **Conference:** Speaker-led event where the primary reason for delegate attendance is to hear from a range of experts or industry stakeholders regarding the latest news, insight and developments in a specific industry. Smaller exhibitions may take place around a conference venue from leading suppliers to the industry.

- **Vertical trade show:** Focuses specifically on an industry attracting only suppliers and exhibitors within a particular industry; e.g., automotive manufacturing show that only features those exhibitors who have a product or service which is used in the supply chain for making cars.

- **Horizontal trade show:** A broader show focusing on a wide range of industries that may be of interest to a general population; e.g., a regional business show that features a range of exhibitors over various industries attracting visitors with a wide range of interests.

## Who?

In selecting the most effective trade show to meet your aims it will help if you can match the attendees with the ideal customer you want to attract. Any event organiser should be able to give you detailed information on who attends their shows (and if they can't you should really question the quality of their data). This gives you an idea of their visitor's general nationality, buying responsibility, type of organisation, etc., which will help you determine whether that's an audience you're interested in or not. By understanding who you want to meet and engage with, you should be able to align whether the audience of a specific show will bring you what you're looking for. Additionally, you may want to consider the size of the audience that a show attracts. It is tempting to invest in a show that quotes the biggest audience, although these can often be the most expensive. A note of caution, however; quoted audiences are just that and past performance is no guarantee of future success so just because an event organiser says they have '20,000 registered' visitors it doesn't necessarily mean they will get 20,000 through the door. If you want to know more about an event's visitor numbers don't be afraid to ask the organisers. If they're doing a good job of getting people through the door they shouldn't be afraid of sharing the details with you. And don't always discount the smaller events, these may be more economical and if they're less busy this may give you a better opportunity for deeper conversations with visitors.

A great source of insight into which events might be most appropriate for you are your existing customers – consider asking them which their 'cannot miss' events are. Quite often exhibitors focus only on meeting new prospects at trade shows, completely forgetting about their current contact base. Trade shows provide a fantastic platform for showcasing your latest product or service and building relationships with customers, as well as demonstrating your investment in the wider industry. The opportunity for your senior team to meet several contacts in one place over a couple of days can be massively more efficient than trying to organise individual one-to-ones in the field. Equally, busy stands always attract more people – we're generally pretty nosey people in business and scared of missing out, so if you invite existing customers to your stand it all helps to make it look busier and attracts more passers-by. Referring back to our previous point about exhibiting where your competitors are, it's worth researching which events they are investing in to see whether there is any potential for your business.

*The quality of attendees was ranked above the numbers attending a show when looking at how to select the right event according to research carried out by CEIR: The Changing Environment of Exhibitions with a score of 84%.*
(Thimmesch, 2013)

## Where?

These days international events are much more achievable (see Chapter 7) and the opportunity to sell to global markets is more attractive than ever. Before you take the plunge and sign up to exhibit abroad, however, remember that the majority of visitors to most shows will be from the domestic market. If you're not able to service the market, or if the market doesn't exist in the country you're looking to exhibit in, then it's worth seriously considering whether that's the right trade show for you. If you decide to exhibit at an international trade event you will also need to clarify exactly who you're looking to connect with at the event – is it a distributor or agent or are you looking to service the market yourself directly? It is also worth considering which markets international visitors are coming from and whether you have the resources to service these markets – if 40% of visitors are coming to a show in Europe are from South-East Asia but you don't have the capacity to service that location, would it be worth you investing in a show that for 40% of visitors you cannot supply? Aside from just the implications of visitor origin, there's also significant additional cost and complexity involved in exhibiting at shows outside of your domestic market, so any investment needs to work harder than ever.

## How?

In researching potential trade shows it's useful to understand how the event organisers advertise and recruit visitors and how hard they are going to work on your behalf. Event organisers want you to have a successful event as it increases your likelihood of rebooking, as well as acting as an advocate to other organisations in your network – so don't be afraid of asking relevant questions. Organisers should be happy to share what they're planning on doing and how they'll get people through the door, as it's all part of the package you're paying for. If they're reluctant to talk about what their marketing plan is or give your vague references about campaigns it might be worth questioning whether they are a partner you want to work with. It's worth reviewing who their previous exhibitors were and even asking for contact details so you can get some feedback from companies who have previously exhibited. GDPR regulations permitting, if you can get the details of a couple of visitors to speak to about their experience and what they are wanting from the show this will also add insight to your decision.

Reviewing the list of speakers at an exhibition will give you a good indication of the how well the event is respected within the industry – are the speakers likely to be of interest to or influence the type of customers you're hoping to meet at the show? If it's not in the public domain then ask the event organiser to send you through the seminar programme and speaker bios of previous events – if nothing else, this gives you details of industry leaders that you might want to contact ahead of the show and invite to your stand if you do exhibit. In these initial engagements with an event organiser you should also get a sense of their culture and how supportive they are going to be in helping you achieve your objectives. In the budget planning section, we will talk more about how you can stretch your budget through asking for added value elements such as speaker slots on live features, or inclusion at networking events and these initial discussions with organisers will give you a flavour of how open they are likely to be to such requests. All good quality event organisers will be keen to work in collaboration with you to help you achieve your objectives rather than just sell you space – after all if you add value to their show by being creative, it all benefits their visitors.

In addition to the general marketing campaigns that the event organisers will run, it is also useful to research who the media partner is. If there isn't one, this eliminates another channel through which you can publicise your participation in the show and it is worth questioning why the relevant trade publications aren't covering the event – is it not seen as credible, is it not newsworthy? If there is a media partner this gives you a fantastic opportunity to speak to a broader audience about why they will benefit from coming to see you at the show as well as driving brand exposure to a much wider audience (see Section 3.8, pre-show marketing).

Researching a show is going to take a bit of time and some clever questioning of the event organisers, customers and previous exhibitors but if you are thinking about investing significant sums of money then you want to be sure you're investing it where you have the highest potential returns... which brings us neatly onto budgets!

### 3.3 Budget planning

We may have mentioned it before, but trade shows cost money, there's no escaping the fact. When it comes to budgeting it's not about how much money can you save, but ensuring you have a realistic budget in the first place and making every single penny work as hard as it possibly can. Trade shows aren't the place to cut costs as it will show in every element and reflect on your brand image, but they are the place to get creative and find efficient solutions.

*Most of a trade show budget is spent by the marketing function of a business. However, few company marketers have had formal trade show or lead generation training and 38% turn to colleagues for the best information on how to do their jobs better – Source: Tradeshow Week Magazine survey.* (Skyline, 2010)

Trees provide a useful analogy to think about budgeting for trade shows in demonstrating the amount of invisible cost that goes into delivering an event. Yet only with solid roots and investing in some of the non-visible elements can the branches and leaves flourish.

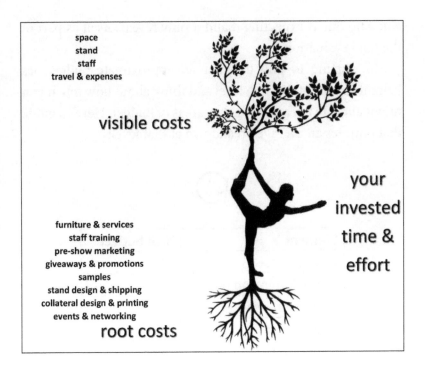

space
stand
staff
travel & expenses

**visible costs**

**your invested time & effort**

furniture & services
staff training
pre-show marketing
giveaways & promotions
samples
stand design & shipping
collateral design & printing
events & networking
**root costs**

Whether you're a business owner setting your own budget or working in an organisation and having to influence a senior team to invest, it's crucial to consider the root costs that can all have a huge impact on your show delivery and hence your return. For example, if you don't take the time to train your team on the SMART objectives, stand operations and opening lines, how will they know what they're trying to achieve and how to engage with visitors. Equally, you may design a high-impact and engaging stand but if you don't factor in any costs to transport or build it, how do you intend to get it from the warehouse to the show floor? Businesses don't react well to surprises or uncertainty so in ensuring that you have all the elements factored into your budget you're at least informed, even if it is a scary number. And it's a much scarier number when no one is expecting it and it only reveals itself as part of the final evaluation.

In starting to pull together an approximate budget, it's helpful to start at a macro level and think about how much you might allocate to each of the key areas of budget. Here's a guide that outlines an average breakdown at that level:

| Element | % of budget |
| --- | --- |
| Buying space | 30% |
| Stand design and build | 25% |
| Additional services | 10% |
| Staff and travel | 20% |
| Promotional | 10% |
| Miscellaneous | 5% |
| Total | 100% |
| Contingency | 20% |

## Buying space

The next section will focus on the process of booking space and how you can add value to your budget in this area. On average the rates for booking space at UK events are around £300 per square metre and shell schemes around £350–£400 per square metre. For more detailed explanations of shell and space options jump ahead to the next section, but shell schemes often come with a number of additional features such as walls, lighting, power, etc., making them more expensive than just buying the physical space. If you're considering investing in space only, the overall cost of delivering the whole show is often estimated at around three times the cost of the space. For example, investing in a 5m × 4m space at a rate of £300 per square metre = 20 × £300 = £6,000. Therefore, the budget expectation for delivering at this scale could be around £18,000, giving you a grand total of £21,600 including a contingency element.

For shell schemes, the average spend is roughly double the cost of the space. For example, investing in a 3m × 3m shell at £375 per square metre = 9 × £375 = £3,375. Therefore, a total budget expectation for delivering at this scale could be around £8,100 including your contingency pot.

## Stand design and build

Again, we will discuss some of the elements to consider when briefing an agency on developing your presence at the show, but from a budgeting perspective it is sensible to allocate around 25% of your funds for this. Even if you are investing in a shell scheme it's important to invest in creating graphics boards and displays that reflect your brand personality professionally. We've seen A4 print outs stuck to dirty grey wall panels and they really don't look impressive. This chunk of budget also mentions 'Build' as we've worked with clients who blew all their cash on creating beautiful stands but had to sacrifice a member of staff on the stand as their travel and accommodation expenses covered the shipping and building of the stand that wasn't in the original costs (and yes this is bad practice from the agency who didn't include these costs in their proposals).

## Additional services

The one that always catches exhibitors out and ends up becoming a money pit if you leave it to the last minute.

Depending on what you negotiate when you're booking your stand you may or may not get a whole range of services such as power, electrics, flooring, furniture, etc., included in your package (more often than not, it isn't included). Equally you may design a stand incorporating the latest tech that requires good broadband access without realising this is all to be paid for. There are a whole host of things that crop up under 'additional services' that you might need, and if you leave it until the day before the show opens they can cost you up to 20% more than booking in advance.

## Staff and travel

Just to be clear we're not talking staff salaries here as this is just about the costs you need to add into your physical budget, but don't underestimate that's a less visible cost to the business. However, if your staff do require additional or enhanced payments for working weekends/Bank Holidays, these and any associated costs will have to be accounted for within your budget. As good practice some organisations also include any costs associated with backfilling essential roles vacated by stand members while at the show as this is a legitimate cost to the business.

If you're not sure how many staff you need, a good estimate is one person per eight square metres with an absolute minimum of two. So, taking our 20 square metre example from above, the ideal number of people would be two or three and with nine square metres you would need two. In addition to the on-site costs of travel and accommodation, it's worth allocating some cost within this budget for staff training – even if that's only two of you, take the time to review your plan before arriving on-site. Any more than four members in your team and it's worth getting everyone together in one place around two weeks prior to the event for a full briefing.

## Promotional

As much as the event organisers will work hard to get visitors through the door, it's your job to get them to your stand. We'll talk in more detail later about pre-show and at-show marketing, but it is advisable to allocate some funds for this, whether it's creating giveaways for the stand or placing adverts in relevant trade magazines. Thankfully in our digital age there's a lot that can be done for free (apart from the cost of time) on social media and with online marketing that can help you and save money on this element. Included in this section would be any samples (including transportation costs) you plan to distribute and the cost of any promotional activity or deals you will be running.

## Miscellaneous

Having a miscellaneous line in your budget just gives you some breathing room for 'stuff' that will inevitably come up, such as a networking dinner or client entertaining, additional venue charges, etc., that you can plan for but don't know about until you start really getting into the finer detail of the preparation.

## Contingency

We're suggesting 20% contingency, which is an absolute ideal. If you can only stretch to 10% then it's still a great safety blanket for when your new MD decides he wants to attend all four days and needs accommodation at the best hotel in town (it happens) or when one of your staff drops the iPad on the first day and you need to replace it to actually capture all the brilliant prospects you're meeting (this also happens). The most frustrating use of contingency we've experienced is when a major, global food producer with a well-known brand created an amazing ice-cream parlour as the heart of their stand. In 2019, if you book power it is usually for 24 hours but there were times when you had to be sure you ordered a round the clock supply otherwise the electricity to your stand got switched off at 6pm. Unfortunately, the exhibitor hadn't read the Exhibitor Manual and didn't book 24-hour power and despite a massive budget and an impressive stand, they were serving milkshake instead of ice-cream on day two of the show. They had been delighted with themselves that up until the show opening they hadn't spent any of their contingency – it soon disappeared as they went about ordering new show stock via a rapid overnight courier and paying for additional power (at a 20% premium above the pre-show booking rate!). Things will crop up, things will go wrong, that's just exhibitions, but with enough planning and some contingency you should be able to sort them out relatively easily and cheaply.

Once you have worked through your estimated total investment and allocated costs to each of the elements then it's time to start really drilling down into the detail of where you'll be spending your money. If you've bought this book alongside *The Exhibitionist Project Manager Journal* we've included some budget templates in there that should help you start to plan how and where you're going to spend your money – but keep it flexible as things will change. After the show, it's always worth hanging onto your budget trackers both for evaluation purposes and reviewing what you need for trade shows in the future.

## Money pits

There are ways you can really waste money on trade shows so here are our five key watch-outs to help avoid wasting budget on non-value adding activity:

1. **The last-minute service orders:** Power, furniture, lighting, etc. will all cost significantly more once you get on-site, or even when you've missed the deadlines! Understand what you need early on and get it ordered at the best (early bird) rates.

2. **Consumables:** Most event venues will offer basics such as cleaning materials, wipes, paper cups, etc., all of which you'll be able to buy much cheaper from local stores. If you're taking your own stand, lob a hygiene box in the car with a few essentials for wiping down at the end of the day. If an agency is building your stand, ask them to pack the essentials on the lorry and bring it with them.

3. **Unnecessary tech:** Everyone loves playing on the latest gadget but before you invest in expensive tech think about what value it adds for your visitor. How relevant is it to you brand? Does it make sense and offer a benefit to your prospects? If it doesn't and it's just being included because you think it's cool, bin it (hypothetically speaking not physically!).

4. **Rigging:** Venues will be happy to charge you to hang banners from the ceiling or fly your flag from unusual spaces but it's expensive. And how many visitors will really see them, bearing in mind they're usually always focused on the stands themselves? If you really want to drive some creative visibility outside of your stand, talk to the event organisers who usually have loads of ideas but choose the

ones without the expensive execution costs. If the flag/ banner idea is still the best option for your brand, then don't be shy in negotiating on the price.

5. **Stick to the rules:** The most expensive and inexcusable waste of resource is when you put all your time, money and effort into creating a fantastic stand, but no one has checked the Exhibitor Manual for the permissions and you arrive on-site to find they won't allow your triple decker, revolving showpiece to be installed. It doesn't happen often, but health and safety managers can and do refuse permission for stands to be built on-site (no matter how big the brand) and there's nothing an exhibitor can do but reload the lorry and head for home without engaging with one single visitor. Rules can be bent but very rarely can they be completely broken, especially when visitor and exhibitor safety is in play.

*Thirty-nine per cent of event planners said that escalating trade show costs and budget/resource management are their biggest challenge – Source: Chief Marketing Officer Council and Exhibit and Event Marketers Association.*
*(Sang, 2017)*

Budgeting is one of the most contentious issues around trade shows, largely because much of the cost may not be visible to those who haven't been involved in the detail of delivering it. Often companies try to make the budget look smaller, because there's such suspicion about being able to calculate ROI – the smaller the budget the lower the returns need to be to make it look like a commercially sound initiative. However, having set SMART objectives there shouldn't be any fear in clearly documenting how much will be needed to achieve them so that all the relevant stakeholders are aware of the scale. As we've said before, no one likes surprises, but visitors can spy a poorly funded and executed presence at a trade show and how long will it take for that negative perception to be repaired, if at all?

### 3.4 Buying your space

You've decided which show you're going to attend and how much budget you're planning to invest, so now down to the serious business of where on the show floor your bucks will work the hardest for you. Before we get to that we want to address a question we're often asked about 'early bird discounts' and 'last-minute deals' – i.e., when's the best time to book your stand to get the best price. As with most questions relating to trade shows and exhibitions, there's no right or wrong answer and much will depend on your objectives and circumstances. We'll talk about evaluation in Chapter 5 and how you decide whether to rebook at the same show in a year's time, but the earlier you can book your space the better – you'll have more time to prepare, have more flexibility to speak to organisers about additional opportunities and you'll have a better selection of available space to pick from. Undoubtedly, event organisers might offer you space at the last minute at reduced rates, but these are unlikely to be the in the best positions on the show floor and if you don't have time to maximise your participation in the show then it could be wasted investment no matter how good the deal looks. If you're clear about what you're looking to achieve from an event and how much money you have to invest then it shouldn't matter too much when you book your space.

Before you get carried away with choosing your space, it's worth having a detailed conversation with the sales manager from the event company to explain your objectives to them and any ideas you have about the added value you might want from the event. This will make it much easier for them to propose which space would be most suitable for you based both on what you're trying to achieve and what is realistic for your budget. It is only wasting both yours and the sales manager's time to discuss spaces that are outside your budget, so be open and honest about what you have available from the first chat. There might be some room to move, but rates are rates and where you are likely to get more value is negotiation on added-value items such as participation in expert panels or additional invitations to networking events for your customers.

The average rates per square metre were detailed in the budgeting section above and give an indication of what you might expect to pay for the size of your stand. However, there may be some instances where those rates are more expensive – for example, when a premium venue is being used to align to a particular industry – or they may be significantly less – for example, if a company is launching a new event or are themselves new in the market. The sales manager will be able to provide you with all the details of the floorplan, current bookings, package deals for marketing and services and a list of the inclusive items you will receive as part of your booking. Most event organisers are happy to show who else has booked space on the event where they can – this is important for you in the decision-making process to ensure your co-exhibitors are the right sorts of businesses that your customers would also be interested in. However, if an event organiser is reluctant to share details about who has already booked into an event it may be due to commercial sensitivities, but it's worth asking about why this is their position and what's stopping them – it might be a lack of bookings.

## Shell vs space only

One of the first questions which a sales manager is likely to ask you is whether you are buying 'space' or a 'shell', which has caught out so many new exhibitors. When exhibitors say they're wanting to book 'space' at a trade show they often mean a shell stand space on the floorplan but a sales manager may interpret this as space only, i.e., just the physical square footage on the plan, no walls, no fascia board, no lighting. It's a really subtle point of vocabulary but so many times we have seen exhibitors turn up having booked 'space' with beautiful graphics panels but nothing to hang them on and just a few business cards to hand out for the duration of the shows. So, to be absolutely clear:

- **Space only:** A physical area of space on the floor where you must provide absolutely everything you need (power and lighting, etc. to the space can be organised through the organisers).

- **Shell:** A pre-built modular construction which may consist of one, two or three walls bordering neighbouring exhibitors for which services such as power, lighting, furniture, etc. can be pre-arranged (usually for an additional cost but always check the Exhibitor Manual). Quite often in the UK these shells are 3m × 3m with three walls unless you get an end location, which typically has two or even just the one wall.

So which space should you book? Consider the floorplan below and without reading ahead pencil in where you think the best position would be for your stand.

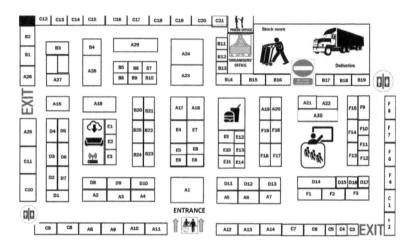

So where did you choose? Quite often stand A1 gets chosen by people who are buying space only and want to make a big impact on visitors as they walk through the door. Sometimes C18 can be chosen by exhibitors who want to be visible as visitors walk up the aisle and who are saving the best for last (we admire their optimism).

Here are some things to consider and then go back to the plan and see if your selection is still the same.

- **Early entry stands:** Visitors tend to be quite over-awed when first entering a trade show and focus on getting their bearings. This can mean that they miss some of the very early stands immediately through the entrance. That's not to say don't book these stands but your stand, content and delivery just need to work extra hard to grab attention. If you have a big message, a good budget and confident staff this can work well but it has challenges.

- **Corner stands:** These stands share traffic where two aisles meet, and therefore should drive twice the number of visitors to your stand. There are also fewer walls for you to create graphics for helping your budget go further – in some instances, if you take the whole of the end of an aisle then it's just one graphics wall.

- **Avoid back walls:** Some visitors will never make it as far as the outer walls and therefore traffic flow can be low. Some event organisers might offer these stands at reduced rates but again it is worth considering whether this is a good use of budget if you're not going to attract as many visitors.

- **Close to the action:** Quite often there are natural areas of busyness – such as live theatres, food and drink concessions and networking/Wi-Fi lounges. These are good spots for your stand as the traffic flow can be stronger – although be aware that visitors may be on their way to something else (e.g., a live session, meeting a colleague) so your team will need to be well trained in grabbing their attention (see Chapter 4). Toilets are always a contentious area… but everyone needs to pay a call sometime so nearby can be a high traffic area, again sensitive management by your team may be required but if the person on a 'mission' has a friend in tow they may fill their time by browsing the nearest stands.

- **Right is right:** Research has shown that visitors tend to naturally veer to the right when they first navigate events such as trade shows so if you can secure a space on the right-hand side you may be able to engage with visitors before trade show fatigue sets in.

- **To compete or not:** Deciding whether to be close or not to your competition is always a difficult call and one that only consideration of your specific circumstances and objectives can answer. The scale, USP, age, budget (and various other factors) of your competitors will determine whether you can shine as a better solution for visitors with a common interest in your products or whether you'll be dwarfed by their size and proposition. It's also worth thinking about complementary exhibitors who sell products or services that could be used in conjunction with your own and book space near them. For example, if you're at a health and safety show and exhibiting a range of secure First Aid storage cabinets you could position yourself next to a supplier of First Aid supplies such as bandages, medicines, eyewash, etc. – if visitors are going to be buying their products they're going to need somewhere to store them. You could even run a joint promotional deal during the show or a competition to win a cabinet stocked full of essential supplies.

- **Grabbing headlines:** If you're looking to secure some big interviews and media coverage as one of your objectives, selecting a location close to the press office might help you achieve it. If you've run an effective pre-show marketing campaign with the media (see below), telling them you're on their way to the press office will make it more likely they'll make the effort to come and see you, than if you're a long walk away!

Did your preferred space change based on some of the considerations we've discussed above?

On the plan below, we've highlighted the areas which in general would be considered as hot spots:

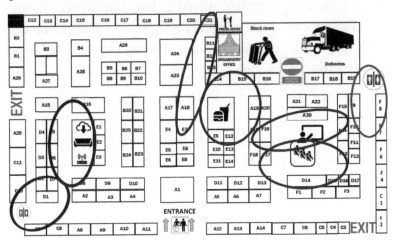

Which space is the best for achieving your objectives will depend on whether you're looking to meet high number of new contacts or need a quieter space where you have time for more in-depth conversations and demonstrations with fewer visitors. Having planned your budget, you will be sure of how much you have available to spend on securing space on the show floor and while it's always worth negotiating with sales managers there's usually not much room for manoeuvre. As we have mentioned, where you do have an opportunity to ensure your budget works harder is thinking about creative added value additions that could improve the event for you and their visitors or save them some time or money. Some examples we've seen put into practice at trade shows include:

- An alcoholic drink exhibitor offering a stocked bar for the networking lounge. This ensured that any visitors using the lounge were only drinking their brands (excluding competitors) and the brand logos were used in marketing collateral, invitations and previews for the show, driving awareness among all visitors.

- A technology supplier offered to loan plasma screens and tablets for the event's Digital Zone, which was then branded with their logos and used in marketing collateral across all the event's platforms.

- An exhibitor was able to secure a larger space than their budget allowed by committing to bring five high-profile contacts to the trade show dinner using tickets provided free of charge by the event organisers. These contacts worked in businesses that could have benefited from exhibiting at the show and the sales manager was able to convert three of these five leads to bookings following the dinner.

Trade shows can be seen as transactional with sales managers interested only in selling square metres. This may have been a fair reflection of relationships in the past but good quality event organisers will be more interested in developing a collaborative partnership that helps you achieve your objectives and adds interest to their show. Not only does this mean they have more satisfied visitors, if you have a good show it's more likely you'll rebook for the following year. Don't think about the buying process as a stand-off between who can win in the rates negotiation – if you think more creatively about how you can extend your reach beyond the space you buy and add value for the organisers, you're much more likely to achieve your objectives.

## 3.5 Stand design

Having decided to invest in a show and booked a space, stand design is quite often the next element that exhibitors jump to and where they almost always end up spending most of their subsequent time and effort. When you consider it takes just a tenth of a second to form an opinion of a business based on their stand and 94% of that opinion is based on the design its clear why this is one of the most crucial elements to get right (Laja, 2018). However, it is just one element of a much bigger path to success and if it isn't aligned to all the other components it can look contrived and confusing.

*According to published research, people form an opinion on whether they can trust someone in one-tenth of a second. Other researchers have found that visitors form an impression of the visual appeal of a website in one-twentieth of a second. So how long does it take for your customer to form an opinion of you and your stand?*
*(Ellett, 2010)*

It's also the element that typically generates the most heated debate, being one of the most visible parts of the budget. While everyone will have an opinion, objection or improvement, there is rarely an absolute right and wrong in terms of stand design, there is just opinion. However, what will keep you grounded as you consider the look, feel and mechanics of your stand is to keep reverting to the overall objectives – what are you trying to achieve and how does it relate to the wider marketing strategy. If the design truly commits to your brand personality and facilitates a conversation that contributes to delivering your objectives, it will be as 'right' as it can be (although there may never be pleasing some of your colleagues). It's worth remembering at this point that what attracts someone to your stand at a show isn't necessarily the same thing that will convince them to buy from you – your stand needs to tempt them in for a conversation, your solution to their problem will lead to them becoming a customer.

## Old versus new

If you already have a stand ask yourself, is it fit for purpose, does it have the potential to meet your current and future needs, requiring only minor reconfiguring or new graphic boards? Or is the construction so far gone that only a skip could handle it? The general rule of thumb is that you'll get three to five years of use from a good stand. But what if your strategy changes mid-lifespan, you have new products that aren't represented or it's looking tired before its time? Whether to keep your exhibition stand, refurbish it, or simply scrap it can depend on a number of factors. You need to determine if scrapping the old stand is financially viable or if your current cash flow says no, then how best do you update it?

**Caution:** big numbers ahead! We know the cost of exhibition stands can range from several thousands of pounds, to a few hundred but we're trying to help everyone, so we know some of you will be over-awed by the numbers we're using here. It's absolutely not a competition, but some organisations do merit investing biggest sums on stand design so bear with us. To help you decide on old versus new you may need the support of your finance department to figure out what the net value of your stand is after depreciation has been taken into account. If you bought the stand from new and it was worth £50k and the depreciation has accounted for £30k then the structure is still worth £20k.

Can you justify binning it or can the structure be reused saving you £20k on the initial rebuild costs?

If your stand is looking tired, old and has no monetary value on the balance sheet anymore then this gives you more room for negotiation to get a good budget to take a new design on. While you are on speaking terms with the finance department, they will hopefully be able to advise you on the annual show budget, which will ultimately determine your course of action around the new versus refurbished debate. Remember also that some elements of your old build may be worth something to someone or can still be reused in a totally new design of your own.

Disposal fees can vary depending on local restrictions as well as the amount of recycling involved. Certain components, such as electronics, appliances, batteries, fluorescent bulbs, among other things, and the transportation of them to special recycling centres for disposal can be hidden charges that you weren't initially considering, but which need to be accounted for. It's always good to ask your current stand builder if they have a buy-back option on any of the components (always an option to consider when ordering a future stand) especially if they are able to strip valuable elements such as aluminium supports from your stand which they can then sell on.

If you plan to use your stand for only a handful of shows over the course of a few years, then it is best to refurbish it since it's only going to be collecting dust in storage somewhere for the majority of its existence. If it's going to be used regularly and can be reconfigured for different sized spaces, it's better to build a new one, particularly if it will enable you to make cost savings via lighter materials, which require less storage and handling charges, thus subsequently recouping some of your build costs via each event. If the structure is sound and meets the core purpose of the required finished product, a hybrid solution combining old and new may be the best option.

Having gathered the required financial and practical information concerning your old design this doesn't mean that you have a green light to go ahead with your ideas for a new one. You need to gather in estimates and a feasibility report on how your ideas could come to life, so you can present your findings and recommendations to internal stakeholders. Even if you are the business owner, going through this process will encourage you to get the best outcome for your brand and convince you, or otherwise, of the benefits or folly of your proposal.

## Stand design agency versus do-it-yourself

No matter if you need a new stand or you've decided to upgrade the old one, one of your first decisions will be whether to use a stand design agency or create and build your own structure. This will largely be directed by what type of area you have booked on the floorplan and whether or not you want a modular solution to cover different events. If you have opted for space only, it is unlikely that you will be able to create a high-quality, engaging and interactive space in your garage (unless your side business is in making theatre props or installing kitchens). Space only can be incredibly exciting in giving you a blank canvas to create a proposition that is truly reflective of your brand and delivers every practical element you need to engage with visitors. It's also really hard to achieve if you're not familiar with the latest materials, tools and technology to bring your ideas to life. On almost every occasion where space only has been booked it's advisable to appoint a reputable and qualified design agency who will help you navigate any construction challenges, advise on minimising build and breakdown times and give you the best possible platform to attract the right types of visitors. We will discuss costs implications in more detail later, but as we have mentioned before there is little point in investing time, money and resource in a show to then deliver a stand that doesn't motivate and inspire both your team and visitors.

For exhibitors booking a shell scheme using a stand design agency may also be the right option to create the most engaging space for your brand, but there is an opportunity to still create a high-impact presence but with less sophisticated equipment. There is a huge range of pop-up display units, fold-out stands and graphics panels that can be used efficiently and effectively to create a quality look and feel for your brand. However, to do these well you'll still need some professional help and budget – a couple of homemade posters hung on the wall and a black-and-white A4 take-away are probably not the greatest reflection of the quality and value you can add for a potential client.

Whether you're deciding to use a stand design agency or a printer with expertise in exhibition equipment, there is a huge selection of suppliers and it can be difficult to choose who to work with. Event managers will often have a preferred agency that they suggest exhibitors work with so it's always worth exploring their costs and experiences – however, they may not be the most creative, or familiar with your specific industry. When visiting exhibitions yourself, take note of any stands that you think are particularly impressive or busy and ask the stand staff who they work with – referring to their work and what you liked about it will massively help a design agency understand what you're looking for. Referrals and recommendations are also helpful as colleagues are unlikely to suggest anyone who they have experienced issues with so ask around your peer group or contact previous exhibitors to the show for their suggestions.

Once you have a short-list it's worth contacting them to ask for case studies and samples of their work, as well as details of their current clients whom you could contact to speak with. During these early engagements, pencil in some time with both the account management and creative team for a coffee and see how you get along with them. You're going to spend a reasonable amount of time engaging with them over the coming months and need to know that you're comfortable to laugh, cry, challenge, listen and endure late nights with them – if they have fantastically creative ideas but you can't stand being in the same room as them then they're not the agency for you. An early flag to watch out for with any agency is whether they're talking in detail about a specific piece of technology, modular system or process that they are planning on using. It could be that they have invested in expensive tech that they now need to make pay for itself regardless of whether it's the right solution for your space or not. If your initial conversations are spent with them mainly telling you how brilliant their kit is without asking questions about what you're wanting to achieve it might be worth exploring other opportunities. Likewise, if a printer or stand supplier is only offering you one type of pop-up or banner solution without understanding your needs it's time to look elsewhere.

## Budget planning

*The simplest definition of a budget is telling*
*your money where to go.*

—Tsh Oxenreider, *Organized Simplicity: The Clutter-Free*
*Approach to International Living*

Before we get more deeply into the detail of briefing an agency, it's time to talk cold, hard cash. Being open and honest with your agency or supplier upfront about what you've got to spend will save you lots of time in the future and ensure that you get what you want and what you can afford. As a writer, there's this gorgeous little Montblanc Peggy Guggenheim Limited Edition Fountain Pen available for a mere £6,800 that I've got my eye on. At the rate I lose and chew pens I probably have £3 for five Bic biros in my budget. Montblanc aren't going to sell me any of their pens for £3, but the little Bic versions do the job just fine, although occasionally if I'm going to an important meeting I'll push the boat out for a £7 Parker rollerball.

The key here is that you'll get what you pay for and a good agency will work hard to make your budget go as far as it possibly can, but they can't deliver you a £25,000 stand for £5,000 – and neither should they. There's a whole host of experts involved in designing, building, shipping, operating and storing your stand. Their skill will create something that works hard to drive your objectives and their expertise could be the difference between engaging visitors and converting leads and not speaking to anyone of value for the duration of the show. Honestly declaring what you want to invest in and what you want to achieve from your stand is the best way of ensuring that your agency partner can create the most effective and efficient solution for you – implying you have £25,000 when really you have £5,000 and are living in hope you'll knock them down on price later just wastes everyone's time, money and effort.

## How to write a stand brief

Once you've decided which stand design agency or print supplier you're going to use, you need to brief them on what you want. A clear, concise and specific brief to work to will always generate a solution aligned to your objectives. Whether you're investing £50,000 in a reusable, bespoke build from scratch or £500 in a pop-up stand, the clearer you are about what you want, the more likely they will be able to deliver it.

So, what do you include:

- **Brand strategy:** briefly, how the trade show fits into your overall strategy

- **SMART objectives:** for the show – the job the stand must deliver on

- **Products and services:** you will be featuring at the show

- **Floorplan:** where you are and where you will attract traffic from

- **Stand size:** shell or space, any services already provided, e.g., power, lights, furniture

- **Brand identity:** logo, colours, fonts, images, strapline, etc. (supplied as high-res jpegs)

- **Messaging:** what the priority message is you want a visitor to get walking past your stand (max 6–10 words)

- **Budget amount:** be realistic and honest

- **Budget coverage:** what exactly the budget covers, e.g., design, build, services at the venue (e.g., power, product storage, furniture hire), stand storage, shipping, consumables (if sampling, for example), staff uniforms, etc. – include everything you can think of that this budget will need to cover, don't assume anything. Even if there are elements that your stand design budget won't be covering, e.g., literature, etc., include everything so the agency can get a sense of the scale of your investment

- **Look and feel:** ideas on the style you're aiming for, e.g., relaxed, formal, fun, etc.

- **Show logistics:** dates, venues, build, breakdown, organiser's contact details

- **Mandatory requirements:** storage, office space, presentation/demonstration area, sampling area (including water source), hospitality/bar, literature rack, etc.

- **AV/tech requirements:** equipment that you know you need to use, e.g., laptops, plasma screens, iPads, etc.

- **Previous stands:** what did you like/dislike about your previous stand, what did/didn't work?

- **Examples:** any images/descriptions of other stands you've seen and particularly like/dislike

- Also include any other documents or information that you think will help an agency better understand exactly what you're trying to achieve

Even if you're only briefing a print supplier to design and create a pop-up stand or banners, considering some of these elements (where relevant) will help them ensure that they create something that while efficient, is also highly effective in communication your proposition and attracting visitors.

### What are the rules?
We may have said that there's no exact right and wrong when it comes to designing exhibition stands and while that might be the case there are some definite principles that the industry agrees on as good and bad practice when creating an exhibition stand:

| Your stand should | Your stand shouldn't |
|---|---|
| Stand out, deliver impact and engage visitors quickly | Get lost in the crowd or shrink into the background |
| Be relevant, clearly communicate your proposition and show the solution you provide for your customers | Confuse or mislead visitors about your product or service |
| Be open, welcoming and inclusive | Create barriers, e.g., tables that deter visitors from coming on to your stand |
| Encourage visitors to interact and engage with you, e.g., demonstrations, sampling – use all five senses to attract visitors and deliver memorable and immersive experiences that visitors emotionally engage and learn from | Appear boring, static or lifeless |
| Offer different experiences for different priorities of customers, e.g., basic literature for passers-by through to a welcoming space for an engaged conversation with prospects and leads | Be one-dimensional with the same service, offer and proposition for all visitors |

| | |
|---|---|
| Combine several different engagement techniques including audio, video and traditional print to cater for visitor preferences | Have a one-size-fits-all approach |
| Offer help and solutions – whether that's plenty of staff available for questions, product trials or handouts with frequently asked questions | A hard-sell platform with no emotional attachment |

Stand design can be a hugely subjective and contentious subject and what one person sees as sleek, minimal design, someone else will see as stark and bare. Likewise, one person's preference to ensure they have every single piece of information available that a customer could possibly request will look cluttered and confused to someone else. The trick to ensuring you have a stand that works hard to engage visitors is to go right back to the SMART objectives you set at the start of the process and check that what you're planning contributes to delivering those aims. Putting the customer at the heart of your stand design and truly understanding how you can demonstrate that your product or service provides a solution for them will keep you on the right track.

### To giveaway or not to giveaway?

One of the most frequently asked questions we hear is whether to invest in giveaways for trade shows – do they deliver any long-term value? Do they just get thrown in the bin? The answer should link back to what your specific objectives are and whether they add value and relevance in building a commercial relationship with visitors.

Before you decide, it's worth remembering that the majority of branded of giveaways are kept for more than 12 months after a trade show. If that's on someone's desk and it's covered in your branding they might just call you first next time they need whatever you're selling.

When executed well, the right giveaway can demonstrate your quality, solidify how you can help solve a customer's problem and keep you front of mind with buyers. However, executed badly they can give a perception of poor quality, lacking creativity and be quickly forgotten.

Food and drink giveaways are perfect if it's your product you're serving – if you're not in the food industry, food and drink is quickly consumed and even more quickly forgotten. Just stop for five seconds and think about exactly what an open tub of Quality Street on a telecoms provider's exhibition stand really tells you about how they can solve your network coverage problem. And believe us when we say the age of cupcakes is well and truly over – we've all eaten quite enough dried up, sickly sweet cakes with a little rice paper logo on to last us a lifetime!

But a branded, lorry-shaped USB stick from a parcel delivery provider or branded power bar for charging up your mobile from an energy supplier – now that starts to make more sense. Equally, it doesn't have to be a specific 'product' you giveaway, your organisation's knowledge and expertise might be one of the most valuable things you can give away so think about content that you have to share – for example, user manuals or 'How To...' videos provided on branded USBs. The only caveat with USB giveaways is the increasing number of organisations who no longer allow the use of USB sticks to mitigate the risks of introducing malware and computer viruses onto their systems.

And it doesn't always have to be your product you give away if you can think of a creative way to make it relevant for your customers. For example, a software company was exhibiting at a tech show in Las Vegas – the obvious giveaway would have been a copy or demo of their software. However, they identified their key target audience were early 30s, getting married and thinking about or due to have babies in the coming months. They created branded babygros with cute messages on to give away at the show and encouraged customers to share pictures of their babies wearing them with their community across social media. They gave away over 1,000 babygros with around 600 known images being shared – imagine how many potential users saw those images from 600 original posts across different platforms. The company was inundated with requests for babygros from potential customers they'd never had contact with before! This could have been a disaster had the company not fully understood who their market was and been creative about engaging with them.

Giveaways don't always have to be the same for everyone either. We'll talk about filtering visitors in Chapter 4 but don't be afraid to offer lower-value giveaways at the front of your stand for everyone, with more value-adding and premium items reserved for those contacts with whom you've had a more productive conversation safely tucked away in the rear or storage area.

*A study was conducted by the Advertising Specialty Institute, finding that on average, recipients keep promotional items for 6.5 months after the day they receive it. This is a powerful statistic that proves the long-term influence of your trade show investment. The length of use for each promo item will vary depending on the product (a pen will be tossed away faster than a calendar that will be around for 12 months!). The ASI study showed that 63% of people who were given a product they did not want, ended up giving it away to someone else. So, even if your item doesn't add value to a one attendee, your investment will not necessarily be in vain. In fact, it might have an even greater impact when it's passed along to a friend or family member who didn't attend the*

*trade show. This tiny act of sharing doubles your exposure and allows your brand to reach customers it couldn't previously access.*
*(CRE8AGENCY, 2016)*

## 3.6 The exhibitor manual

It's the phrase that sends a shiver down the spine of so many exhibitors but it's the single most useful document you lay your hands on during the entire exhibition cycle (well apart from this book that is!). Exhibitor Manuals come in all sorts of shapes and sizes from single A4 hard-copy sheets, to downloadable e-books and online portals but whatever format they come in they are guaranteed to have the answer to just about any question you can think of to help you plan, implement and evaluate effectively.

## Where do I get it from?

Most organisers will make their Exhibitor Manual available to you as soon as you've sent them confirmation of your booking. After all, they may have in excess of 1,000 exhibitors on the books so they're keen to give you as much information as possible that avoids them fielding endless phone calls on the same topic. If your sales manager hasn't mentioned this soon after you've booked, then it's worth chasing them up for details – some may be sending you something in the post (becoming less frequent these days) but usually they will send you a link to an online portal where you can find everything you need. For some shows we have seen as many as seven different downloads consisting of 20–30-page documents in each download, which can seem overwhelming. It's therefore not surprising that so many exhibitors give up on the manual before they've really started – but as with researching the right show, it's better spending a couple of hours at the start of the process to really get to grips with the detail than get on-site and find that your triple-decker, revolving stunner of a stand won't get through the door!

## What's in it?

The content of an Exhibitor Manual will vary by event company, industry and country but there are a lot of common elements you can expect to find in every manual:

- **Basic logistical details:** Show opening times, build and breakdown access, venue address, etc. This will tell you when you have access to the venue to build your stand and when it can be taken down. With so many exhibitors, contractors and staff on-site, event organisers have to be strict about when people have access to ensure everyone can get set up in time for the show opening – being respectful of their times and processes is in your best interests. This is also where you'll find all the details you need for getting your kit on-site if you've employed a stand design agency as there are usually booked times or restrictions on when vans can arrive and unload.

- **Badges and passes:** A process for ensuring that everyone who needs to get on-site (e.g., staff, stand builders, etc.) to deliver your event is registered. This might even include car parking passes, which believe it not can be one of the most sought-after pieces of paper at a show!

- **Catering:** If you're looking to host any kind of networking event with drinks and snacks or want to sample or serve any kind of food or drink from your stand, this is where you'll find the rules. Venues can be quite protective about exhibitors offering food and drink at their stands as it could impact on revenues through the venue's own cafés and bars. It can also be quite expensive to serve food and drink at your stand, and noisy, so if you've got 4–5 senior contacts you know will be at the show, consider running an early morning breakfast or evening drinks reception where they're less likely to be distracted.

- **Health and safety:** Crucial to ensuring that your stand can physically be built on-site. Health and safety managers can, and do, refuse to let exhibitors continue if they haven't got the relevant paperwork and authorisation to build a stand – and no they're not being jobsworths, they're just trying to keep people safe. Even if you're arriving with a DIY stand and a laptop, there will still be health and safety considerations you'll need to know about and stick to. There may be forms you need to complete and submit by a certain date, or it may just be a list of rules but if you read nothing else in the manual read this bit!

- **Risk assessment:** Tied into health and safety, the risk assessment document reflects anything about your stand that might hurt, injure or kill someone (even a faulty plug could be a hazard). Even if you don't need to submit your risk assessment it's worth doing it for a couple of reasons. First, the health and safety officer can ask to see it at any time, so you need it on-site. Additionally, it makes you think about how safe your stand is, after all you really don't want your press coverage following the event to be all about how everyone tripped over your stand and injured themselves. If you're serving food samples, have you thought about food allergens and displaying warning notices? If you're using working machinery as part of your display, what could happen if someone stuck their hand in while it was working? If you're showing things on a screen, is there anything in your content that could trigger epilepsy? The worst-case scenarios are unlikely but it's worth thinking about how you can ensure you spend your time having quality conversations with potential buyers rather than fighting fires or administering First Aid.

- **Contractors and services:** Recommended organisations that the event organisers believe to be reliable and reputable whose services you might need. This could be anything from hotels and taxis to furniture and floral arrangements. Especially important for international trade shows, these usually include details of the show's nominated freight forwarder for getting your stand and samples to the show and back again. You may have a suspicion that using the show's nominated contractors will cost more than sourcing your own and you could be correct, but the additional cost is worth the peace of mind that everything you order will be delivered on time and in full. Contractors work hard to gain the trust of event organisers and therefore will be reliable, trustworthy and know intimately how the show and the venue works, which will all help ensure you have the best possible show you can.

- **Deliveries:** Event venues are *huge* spaces and things invariably get lost so wherever possible the advice on deliveries is *don't*! However, things go wrong with timings so if you have no other option than to get a delivery made, check the Exhibitor Manual to ensure you get the right details for your package to arrive at the right show and on time.

- **Power:** Many exhibitors have been caught out in presuming that booking a space or shell includes a power supply and it's not until they get on-site and go to plug in their kit that they realise they have to buy it, and usually at a premium by that point. The Exhibitor Manual will tell you exactly what you have as standard with your booking and how and when to order more at the best possible rates. Ordering a power supply and using an adaptor/4-bar for additional sockets is a cost-effective way of securing more capacity *if* the event organisers allow it, but check the manual to be sure.

- **General rules:** All events vary in what exhibitors can and can't do in terms of alcohol, gas, sampling, distributing literature and a whole host of other areas, so to make sure you're not wasting money on something you can't do, here's where you'll find the rules. Event organisers want their exhibitors to have as good a show as possible, so if there's something you can't do that would significantly enhance your offer and the visitor experience then talk to your sales manager, there may be a way you can collaboratively bend the rules. Breaking the rules is never going to win you any fans and ignorance is no defence.

- **Insurance:** Event organisers are starting to get more stringent in their need to see exhibitor insurance cover to ensure they are protected. For most exhibitors their standard operating insurance policy will cover events such as trade shows so there shouldn't be anything more to do than just make sure you have a copy available in case anyone wants to see it, or worst-case scenario you need it for anything. However, it's worth checking the terms and conditions of your policy – are you covered for this type of activity and do you need to take out additional cover (especially for international shows)? This cover may need to be sourced via a specialist provider in some instances but a call to your normal broker should shed light on this for you, otherwise the myriad of exhibition associations or the show's organisers will help you.

- **Show marketing:** We'll cover pre-show marketing in the next section but one of the easiest and most efficient ways of ensuring potential buyers know you'll be exhibiting at the show is to use every single piece of marketing collateral an event organiser provides for you. There will be a whole host of tools including the show website, press releases, visitor emails and downloadable logos and banners that will all help you and all the details will be in the manual.

- **Permissions:** There are a number of elements such as sampling, using music or playing videos that you might need permission from the organisers for, or a secondary authorisation such as PRS/PPL certificates. The Exhibitor Manual will tell you what you are allowed to do and how to apply for permission. Without the right permissions, again you might turn up on-site and find out that you can't run your stand in the way you want to. When playing video or music, remember to be respectful of your fellow exhibitors and keep the levels at an acceptable level.

- **Contact details:** For organisers, sales managers and operations teams – stick them in your phone early on in your planning then you can quickly and easily get to them whenever you need them.

- **Lead capture:** We'll talk about how to capture leads effectively below but one of the most obvious objectives for a trade show will be collecting new contact details to start building relationships. There are a number of different methods you can use to capture details, from physically collecting business cards to scanning badges or investing in an app that will feed directly into your organisation's CRM system. Which method will be right for you will depend on your objectives and resources for following up after the show. There may be a data-capture device included in the price of booking your stand, or a special offer from the recommended supplier which will be detailed in the Exhibitor Manual.

- **Storage and handling:** If you've built a good storage space in to your stand you may not need any additional space but if you've got multiple samples, additional literature or giveaways that require off-stand storage, this will need booking in advance of arriving on-site. This is particularly important if you have any perishable or frozen goods. Most exhibition organisers won't allow the storage of cardboard boxes on stands as they are considered a fire hazard but be honest, what impression does a load of boxes strewn across your stand give of your brand? Storage space can be booked using the forms you'll find in the Exhibitor Manual including any lifting, moving and handling you will need to get items on to the show floor using forklifts. Be mindful that once the show starts there will be restrictions in place regarding the movement of products to and from the storage area to minimise visitor and exhibitor injuries.

- **Food and drink sampling:** If you're working in the food and drink industry there are very strict regulations about how to sample, who can sample and requirements in relation to waste and water. If your whole stand is built around sampling, it's especially important to read, digest and follow the rules on what you can and can't do.

- **Name board:** For shell schemes this is where you'll find the form to complete to tell the organisers the company name you want to appear on the front of your stand. If you don't complete this, they will either leave it blank or use the name you've put on the booking form, which isn't always the name that customers or the trade would recognise.

- **Wall panels:** Again, for shell schemes this will give the details of the size of the panels for creating graphics boards to hang on the shell walls. You'll need to give these details to your design company or printers so that they can fit your graphics without splitting up words or images. It's no fun hacking into your graphics at the show when you realise they don't fit the walls and don't assume that every shell scheme will have the same dimensions as they quite often don't. It's also worth asking the operations contacts at the event organisers whether your shell scheme will host a junction box, which can again mean you need to hack into your graphics to fit around a big square power supply box.

- **Stand plan/method statement/technical drawings:** For space-only stands, organisers will quite often ask for a number of documents to ensure that what you're planning will be appropriate for the space you've booked and whether there are any additional considerations they need to make during build-up and breakdown. Your stand design agency should be very familiar with dealing with all these elements and you should just be able to leave it with them to sort out.

- **Freight forwarding:** For international trade shows this can be one of the most complex aspects of planning but simply employing the experts to take control of this all for you will ensure that your stock and stand ends up in the right place at the right time. As well as details of the recommended freight forwarder, the Exhibitor Manual will give you details of lead times and logistics for the specific venue. The worst case of an exhibitor getting freight forwarding wrong that we have come across is a humdinger! The exhibitor had booked space only at a show in Asia and thought they could get a better deal on the freight costs than those offered by the official freight forwarder. The original stand was sent out and impounded in Turkey. A second stand was shipped by expensive air freight, so it could get there in time, this one arrived but was so damaged that the organisers wouldn't allow them to build it on-site due to health and safety concerns. Their stock arrived at the destination harbour only to fall foul of a custom clearance issue. So having paid for space, two stands and their stock to be shipped halfway round the world the exhibitor had an empty space and a handful of business cards to give away. Subsequently they had a long time to contemplate what went wrong and the steal their competitors now had on them while they tried to fill in the rest of their time in before they flew home with nothing to show for an expensive four-day trip.

We've given you a flavour of the sort of information you might find in the Exhibitor Manual but there will be so much more that will give you help, support and inspiration specific to the show you're exhibiting at. From reading this section you might have the impression that the manual is there to stop you from doing what you want or tie you up in knots while deploying a mountain of bureaucratic paperwork. But its purpose is to give you all the information you need to make the most of the show and to keep everyone safe (don't forget your high-vis vests for build-up and breakdown!). Exhibitions are big, noisy, busy and complicated affairs and with so many people, variables and potential for things to go wrong it's crucial that event organisers try and find a way for things to run as smoothly as possible.

That said, the manuals can be lengthy and complicated, so it's worth investing the time to create your own tracker containing the details of the specific forms, deadlines, rules and details that you will need to run your show efficiently.

If you've bought this book alongside *The Exhibitionist Project Manager Journal*, we've included some Operations Tracker templates in there that should help you break down your specific Exhibitor Manual and create a timed plan of what you need to do and when to hit all of the major deadlines.

## 3.7 Lead capture

We referenced lead capture above and it's crucial to think about what and how you will collect the key data during the show that enables you to measure the success of your objectives. How you decide to capture contact information will depend largely on what your specific objectives are, what methods are available to you, stand resource and how you intend to use the information you collect. The important element is to have a process and know that your team feel confident in using it.

Some of the methods that are often used at trade shows include:

- **Business card collection:** It's a traditional method but for lots of businesses it still works. It's a quick and easy way for visitors to share their information and the exchanging of cards implies consent for future contact (important in the days of GDPR). However, the information is quite shallow, and it can be difficult to remember who people are when just sorting through a stack of random cards back in the office. It helps to at least categorise cards into priority order such as writing Gold, Silver, Bronze or Contact, Prospect, Lead on each card so you or whomever is processing them at least has some kind of prioritising system to work to.

- **Electronic business card capture:** Most smartphones have apps that allow the image of a business card to be captured and the details transferred to your contacts list. Again, the information collected is reasonably shallow and if you have different squad members using their own phones there has to be a process of collating them after the show, but it does mean no one ends up with a huge stack of cards at the end of the show. If you are collecting details electronically it can be worth taking a quick photo of someone holding their badge at the same time to act as a memory jogger. The problem here is also that your squad will all have their phones in their hands for legitimate reason, which might just prove too tempting when it comes to checking emails and taking calls!

There's still a disturbingly high percentage of exhibitors relying on the so-called 'fishbowl method' of collecting business cards, without any formal lead categorisation process. The only thing you can take from this is that everyone that put a card in wanted to win the prize on offer. Plus, unless you have put a GDPR compliant statement up, you can only contact the winner to arrange for them to receive their prize. Then their card, together with the rest of the business cards you have amassed, need to be securely disposed of as they haven't given you permission to use their details for any other reason. This in our opinion is a waste of time, effort and prize money that could be used on a far better way of engaging with visitors.

- **Data scanners:** Often provided by event organisers (sometimes with an additional fee), exhibitors scan a barcode on the badges of visitors and are then sent a spreadsheet of the visitors' details after the event. Using this method relies on the visitor having given the correct details when registering for the event (many give false details to avoid being spammed) and the questions asked at registration are often based on what an organiser is interested in measuring as opposed to what's useful to an exhibitor. Data captured in this way is one-dimensional and doesn't give exhibitors any opportunity to distinguish between different priorities for visitors, which can mean a lot of wasted time and effort prioritising them post-event. The plus side of this method is that the information collated by the scanner is GDPR-compliant as the visitor will have had to agree to their information being shared at the point of registration.

- **Pen and paper/visitor book:** Still a useful method employed by many exhibitors for recording any specific notes and details about a visitor that have emerged as useful for following up. Templates can be created with a series of set questions that you're interested in getting the answers to which can also act as a framework for the squad to navigate the conversation. Some exhibitors prefer having one book where all contact details are stored along with clips of business cards, although this can be difficult if there's only one book at busy shows. In terms of following up, it could be difficult interpreting different types of handwriting and can be reasonably labour intensive in transferring contact details onto an electronic system.

- **Lead capture apps:** Sometimes offered as a more premium alternative to data scanners by organisers, lead capture apps can be downloaded on most smartphones and enable exhibitors to scan badges using the camera to access visitor details. There are also usually preloaded in-app questions with free-text fields and options to create bespoke information-gathering prompts. Contact details are usually available instantly and held in the cloud for a period of up to about 12 months after the show. If the apps rely on a solid broadband connection this can sometimes be challenging in venues with unstable Wi-Fi (although the better apps store details until they have a connection), and again it is putting devices into the hands of the stand squad.

- **CRM-related apps:** Depending on which CRM system your organisation uses, some offer downloadable apps that link directly into the platform transferring data immediately into your system. This can be of benefit if your squad are already familiar with a system as it negates the need for additional training. Equally, if you regularly communicate with customers via an automated newsletter mail list, these apps can place contact details into the circulation list ensuring that new contacts will automatically hear from you through the newsletter at least. However, these platforms can often be quite expensive making them unrealistic for smaller businesses – but check out if any offer a 14-day free trial which may give you enough time to cover your event and follow-up.

- **Generic lead capture apps:** There are a number of free or low-cost generic apps available for smartphones that enable exhibitors to create their own series of questions to record visitor information. However, these can sometimes be advert-heavy to make them commercially viable, which can slow down the collection process. As with any of the electronic options, these may rely on more technically confident stand members who are used to using similar apps for recording information.

- **Self-recording:** Some exhibitors build tablets and data collection systems into their stand design, which allows visitors to enter their own information and answer a series of questions to identify how they want to be communicated with going forward (GDPR compliant). While this can be an efficient way of collecting data it is relatively shallow as there is no opportunity to engage with and really understand visitor need.

In reality, it is likely that several different methods would be employed at the same event depending on how the conversation develops. If there is no opportunity for a business relationship to develop then there is little point collecting contact details – following up would just be a waste of both of your time. If a visitor has been identified as a contact, for example a supplier, it may be enough just to collect a business card or scan a badge. However, as you start to establish a more developed conversation with an interested browser or definite buyer it's likely you'll want to record more detailed information about their needs and current buying position. This might require either a written record or collection via an app, at which point a stand member who is adept as using your electronic capture method of choice could take over the process.

The methods mentioned will help you capture details of visitors at your stand but trade shows often create opportunities away from the stand where you could meet interesting contacts such as around live events, evening networking dinners and at the bars around the venue, so it's worth having a stack of cards handy in case you meet anyone worth keeping in touch with away from your base.

## What to capture

There are obvious details you'll want to capture such as name, number and email, which will ensure that you can actually contact the prospects and leads that you've met, but have you ever thought about what else you might want to collect that would be useful? In the next chapter we'll talk about filtering visitors so as you progress through that mining process these are some of the details you might want to capture:

- **Their business aspiration:** If a visitor is looking to retire or sell-up soon, is it worth investing time in building a relationship? If they're currently seeking investment does that give you an indication (positive or negative) about what budget they might have available and their ability to pay you?

- **Their problems:** Is there anything they mention that your product can't solve but would be useful to them – this could be valuable innovation for you. Do they talk about anything you hadn't thought of that your product or service solves for them?

- **Route to market:** If you're not going to be selling directly to them, where do they buy from and can they get your product through their preferred channel? If not, is this another distribution partner for you to add to your prospect list?

- **Estimated annual order value:** Don't be shy in asking about how much they think they could buy from you in a year, it will all help ensure you allocate the appropriate resource to them post-show. There's a big difference between a visitor who is going to buy one widget to fix the faulty hinge in his gate, versus the visitor who is looking to equip his 1,000-strong maintenance team with your widgets.

- **Current supply:** Who is currently supplying them and why would they consider changing? Have there been any problems with the current supplier in terms of the product or customer service? This is one to be cautious with as the visitor may just be looking for a competitive price from you, so they can go and renegotiate with their current supplier.

- **Next steps:** How do they want to be communicated with going forward? Each prospect or lead will have a preferred method of keeping in touch and it can help to build the relationship based on how they want you to speak to them. For those really hot leads, make sure you both understand what the next step is and when that will happen so there are no disappointments around failures to deliver.

If you're going to be passing leads onto your sales team for follow-up, it's worth asking them what information they need to enable them to competently pick up the relationship. Their perspective will be valuable in ensuring you're giving them the best ammunition to convert the lead. They might also be able to help non-sales squad members better understand the difference between a lukewarm and a hot lead to enable them to recognise different visitors more quickly.

## 3.8 Pre-show marketing

If you've put all the previous planning steps in place you might be thinking your job's done and you can just sit back and wait for visitors to swarm to your stand, desperate for more information to confirm that yours is most definitely the product or service they've been missing all their life. Equally, you might believe it's the job of the event organisers to get visitors through the door and over to your stand. Neither assumption would be correct and a targeted, consistent and engaging pre-show marketing campaign can be one of the most effective ways to make sure you get exactly the right type of prospects to your stand.

The more engagement you can drive with visitors to get on their 'Must See' list before they even walk through the doors the better. A busy stand always attracts more people so if you can line up appointments it will go a long way to creating a buzz around your stand – existing customers and the media are a great route for securing definite meetings. Think of a quirky and engaging way to attract the people you really want to talk to at the show by making it worth their while to come and see you.

Here's a great example we heard of from an American manufacturer that generated significantly more business than the cost of the initial idea. There were five key buyers that the manufacturer wanted to meet at their industry trade show, but they knew they would be vying for time with their competitors and several high-profile speakers and events around the show. They bought five Montblanc pens at a cost of around £500 each and sent the empty boxes to the five key buyers they wanted to speak to. Along with the empty box they sent a message stating that if they gave up 15 minutes of their time at the show to meet the CEO they would get their £500 pen. All five contacts confirmed an appointment and came along for the meeting, two had agreed in principle to an order before leaving the stand, one agreed to a follow-up meeting after the show and two agreed to keep in touch and explore opportunities in the future. Six months later the business gained from those five customers had more than paid back the cost of the stand and the cost of the pens.

If you don't have a £2,500 Montblanc budget don't panic, there are lots of creative ways you can come up with engaging with a visitor to pique their interest and get on their list, and more importantly there are lots of free ways you can communicate with the whole trade show audience to make sure they know why they'll get value from coming to meet you at the show.

## Event collateral

The event organisers will work hard to get people through the door and in doing so, will create lots of opportunities for you to be part of those communications. Across the weeks prior to the show the organisers will talk to their audience through social media, digital, trade press and direct communications, some even have telesales teams calling visitors who have registered to encourage them to attend. The primary way of getting involved is by ensuring you cover every element that comes as part of your package, which will be detailed in the Exhibitor Manual – this will include items such as a listing on the event website, or in the show guide, downloadable banners for your website or email signatures with some even offering personalised invitations with your branding on to send out to customers. Exactly what's available in terms of event collateral will depend on the show but the event organisers won't chase you for your details to be included in any of those elements – that's all down to you. Getting your details listed on the event website as early as possible always helps as it gives you content to talk about on social media (see below) and it never looks good when your competitor has a shiny logo and a tempting trade show offer, and you've got a big white space next to your company name.

## Social media

Instant, free and scalable social media is a dream platform for communicating with a wider audience about your participation in the show. Not only can you engage with customers, visitors and other exhibitors but you can talk to an audience beyond that to demonstrate your investment and show how you can add value. Trade shows will have their own social media platforms through Twitter, LinkedIn and Facebook, so follow those as soon as you've agreed your participation and be part of the conversation. Like other people's posts, reply to Tweets and LinkedIn with visitors and exhibitors. Try not to 'tell' people just to visit you through your social media posts, become part of the conversation by talking about the show overall, solving other exhibitors' problems and showing how you'll add value for visitors.

We've often seen companies tweet out photos of the team who'll be on their stand creating an emotional connection with visitors who then feel more comfortable approaching the stand when they recognise a face. You could ask for feedback on your stand design and what visitors feel is more engaging for them. If you're a food producer, ask visitors which of your flavours they'd most want to taste or which new variety they'd be interested in seeing at the show. Ask prospective customers what's currently their biggest challenge in the industry and then develop a workshop or talk by an expert at your stand to answer their queries and invite visitors to come along and listen. If there are well-known experts from your industry who are listed on the speaker programmes, connect with them via LinkedIn and publicly invite them over to your stand during the show, but be sure there's something in it for them otherwise they might (publicly) say no! If your website has a blog section write about your experience of planning for the show, who you're hoping to meet and what you're most looking forward to. Never has it been so quick and easy to talk to visitors and your wider audience to engage with them before they even arrive on-site and make sure that they know you're worth visiting. And remember, if you have left your pre-show marketing to the last minute then there's no quicker and more immediate way to engage than through social media – it's the answer to every last-minute Luke's prayers!

*By combining social media and event marketing all year-round leading technology company Cisco boosted clickthrough on their website by 236%.*
(Milloway, 2016)

## Trade media

Your industry media gives you another great opportunity to not only engage with visitors before they get through the doors of the show but also talk to a wider audience of potential customers who might not be able to visit the show. Every show is likely to have a credible magazine as their media partner and if you can get them excited and talking about what you're doing at the show, you're sure to catch the attention of visitors as they plan their day. Trade magazines will run show previews and reviews, and in our experience, they aren't bombarded with content from exhibitors so anything you can share with them will have a good chance of being covered (so long as it's relevant and engaging). Planning ahead will also give you the chance to make sure that every trade advert that's placed in the run-up to the show talks about your presence, stand number and why visitors will benefit from making the time to come and see you. Journalists face as big a challenge as visitors in working out how to make the best use of their time, so if you can engage them before the event by showing how you can provide relevant and interesting content for their readers they're more likely to put you on their list – but don't forget to remind them of your appointment on the day – they're busy people!

If you're not really sure how to handle the media, how to balance paid-for and earned activity and what to say and what not to say, Chapter 6 will give you more detail about how to get the most from your trade media partners.

## Personalised invitations

In this age of digital media and communicating through screens there's nothing like a personal invitation to make a contact feel engaged and loved, increasing the likelihood of them paying a visit to your stand. Whether it's existing customers that you want to invite and say thank you, new targets that you want to be sure make a detour to your stand or journalists that you want to interview your key contact, a personalised and direct approach can make all the difference. Again, the important factor is showing them how they will benefit from a visit to your stand and making it worth their while, but if you've grounded your stand design and proposition in solving their problems this shouldn't cause you any issues. We'll talk about briefing your team in the next chapter but if you are sending out invitations to key contacts it's important to make sure your team know who they are – all that goodwill could be lost in an instant if they turn up and no one recognises them. If you feel that your stand isn't going to give you the right environment to conduct the conversation you want to have, there will be other options around the show. It might be beneficial to organise lunch at a high-quality local restaurant if your contact is a high-value customer. If your aim is to help inform and engage with new contacts who have low awareness of your product or service, a private drinks reception with a short formal talk followed by general networking with your team might be the answer. Most shows will have networking events and awards that you could purchase additional tickets for to invite contacts – the benefit being contacts are more likely to attend an industry event, although you'll be competing for their attention with other exhibitors and distractions. If you have secured a slot on a speaker panel or expert discussion, consider inviting interested contacts or media to come and listen, offering to meet then afterwards for a coffee and discuss the content in more detail. In the world of smartphones and tablets it's easier than ever to drop a quick video invitation to your key contacts, it's more likely to disrupt them and be far more engaging than all the other standard emails they'll receive. If it's important you see them on the day, don't leave it to chance that they stumble across your stand in the midst of all the other competing noise, lights and action! Getting a date and time in the diary is even better!

## Internal and customer communications

Planning a trade show can feel like a thankless and solitary task at times, especially in larger organisations where your colleagues are suspicious of the amount of budget you're investing on a few days' jolly in the sunshine. If only they knew how physically, mentally and emotionally draining exhibitions can be they wouldn't be in such a rush to dismiss it as just another marketing money pit. So in the same way we've talked about grounding all your plans in customer benefits, think about how you can sell the benefits of an effective trade show execution to your colleagues. When they better understand what you're trying to achieve and how it could benefit them they're likely to have more enthusiasm for your plans and shout about them to any of the external contacts they're talking to, hence increasing exposure and awareness of your presence at the show.

Many sales and marketing teams salivate in anticipation of the latest TV advert, promotional plan or new product development that they can go and enthuse about to customers to help them sell. Trade shows and exhibitions may cost as much as some other marketing initiatives but rarely do businesses get as excited about them or how they could positively impact results. Sharing your objectives, stand designs, customer targets and potential returns will help colleagues understand what and why you're investing in live events and what it can mean for them, e.g., more sales, great profits, salary rise, additional bonus, etc.

Hopefully engaging with colleagues and helping them understand the plan will inspire the same excitement as a new product or TV advert and encourage them to talk about it with their own customers and contacts in the industry. By making it everyone's responsibility to promote your presence at the show, you'll inevitably reach a wider audience and get on more visitor's must-see list before they arrive at the show. As mentioned, event organisers will usually provide a whole host of ways for you to include branding about the show (including your stand number) on your customer communications. These may include email signature inserts, banners to go on your website, personalised invitations and show logos. Making these available to everyone in the company again increases exposure beyond your direct circle and drives awareness about your investment in industry events.

## Speaker slots

Getting on the live features agenda at a show can be a valuable way to establish your credibility in the industry and provide content to talk about before and after the show. Different shows have different methods of managing speakers, some pay for professionals, some offer slots for free based on the speaker building their profile and some charge speakers. What every show has in common, however, will be sourcing content that's engaging, relevant and innovative and adds value for the audience. Even if an event is asking speakers to pay for slots, this isn't licence to deliver a boring, hard-sell product pitch to try and drum up some interest in your stand. Having attended and run several live theatres at various events we've seen a whole range of the good, the bad and ugly! The ones that work the best are very light on slides (no slides is the optimum!), relaxed and informal, and feature theory and practice. For example, it may be difficult to make your very technical but super-duper new seven-way widget with extra bells and whistles sound exciting, but get your client talking about the increased efficiency and cost savings to an audience of lean manufacturers and you're onto a winner! If you've become the nation's leading artisan peanut butter cupcake maker, selling millions to Harrods, tell your story to the audience of food entrepreneurs and start-ups and share knowledge that will help them on their journey. If you think you have new insight, knowledge or a story that the show audience would be interested in, it's always worth contacting the show organisers and finding out what the opportunities are. But remember if you do get on the schedule, shout about it – it's gold dust for marketing!

## Summary

Phew, so there's a bit more to it than booking some space and turning up with a couple of pop-up banners and a handshake – well there is if you want to generate some meaningful returns from your exhibition investment. It's never too early to start your planning, the more time you give yourself, the more time you have to think about decisions, take second opinions and make amends to the plan when it's going off track. Equally, the pressure of last-minute decisions can inspire some fantastic creativity and generate high productivity so it's never too late to do something positive that can influence the outcome of your show. So, if you're reading this and your show's tomorrow, even sending one tweet tonight to one of your key contacts might just make the difference between seeing them tomorrow or not!

We've covered a huge amount of content in this chapter (don't worry it gets easier from here on in!) so we thought you'd find it useful if we cover the key points from the last few pages as a checklist of key questions to guide your planning:

- What does success look like for your trade show – what are your SMART objectives?

- Are you attending the show that gives you the best chance of meeting your objectives?

- Does your budget realistically give you enough flexibility to achieve your objectives?

- Have you spread your budget across both visible (branch) and invisible (root) costs?

- Have you picked the hot-spot on the show floor that will give you access to the best quality leads to achieve your objectives?

- Is your stand design grounded in showing visitors how your product or service solves their problem?

- Do you know what the key operational deadlines and rules are for your specific show? Can you meet the deadlines and do all your plans meet the organisers' conditions?

- Do you know which method of lead capture you're going to use and what data you're going to collect?

- Have you created an aligned, consistent and engaging pre-show marketing campaign that targets key visitors and gets your stand on their must-see list?

So that's the first slice of the P.I.E. devoured and digested and now you're fully prepped to turn the show floor into your shop window. All you need now is a fully briefed and capable team who can recognise and filter visitors using opening questions that immediately identify those visitors who can and can't buy from you. Not sure how you go about that? Don't panic, just keep reading! While the next chapter is called 'Implementation', don't leave it until the morning of the show to read it, although it is about what actually happens on the day of the show, there's (even) more planning you'll need to do having read it to ensure a successful opening day!

*There are no secrets to success. It is the result of preparation, hard work and learning from failure.*

—General Colin L. Powell – USA (Ret.)

# CHAPTER 4

# IMPLEMENTATION

*Vision without action is merely a dream. Action without
vision just passes the time. Vision with action
can change the world.*

—Joel A. Barker, technology and business
futurist and author

Having spent months planning how you're going to engage and inspire the target visitors you've enticed to your stand, you're hopefully raring to get on the show floor and start collecting leads. As the above words of wisdom suggest, all the planning in the world counts for nothing unless those plans are converted to action with enthusiasm, commitment and discipline. In this chapter we'll consider how to nail the perfect build on-site, pick your winning squad, engage visitors with stunning opening lines and filter out the time-wasters.

## 4.1 On-site final build
Depending on whether you've selected to work with a stand building agency or you're arriving with your own pop-up kit, the last few hours before doors open are nerve-wracking and exciting in equal measure. As you watch your stand emerge on-site there will undoubtedly be jitters about some of the decisions you've made but think back to the evidence you used to make those decisions, grounded in your customers' key needs and stop doubting yourself. Build days are noisy, busy

and pressurised and very often things don't go according to plan. Most of the problems you come across will have been experienced before by other exhibitors, stand-builders or the event organisers – asking for help and a little negotiation means most problems can be resolved on-site (although it might cost you, so be prepared for last-minute charges).

If disaster strikes and your kit doesn't turn up for whatever reason, it's time to get creative with your solutions. If you're working with a stand design agency, now isn't the time for post-mortems and blame (although you will need to find out later what happened). Do they have other clients' kit that you can adapt and amend for your purpose? What furniture, equipment and graphics resource do the event organisers have on-site that can help you pull together a passable stand in the time you have left? If you're bringing your own kit and it simply hasn't turned up or it's arrived damaged or incorrect, the easiest way for you to dress your stand might be using the everyday branded items you find around your office of workplace. The worst option is not to exhibit – if you've put pre-show marketing plans into place and made appointments to see people, they will expect to see you. You might not have the exact stand you want but a prospect is more likely to be understanding of missing graphics than they are of a missing exhibitor they had arranged to meet.

*Opportunity does not waste time with those*
*who are unprepared.*

—Idowu Koyenikan, *Wealth For All: Living a Life of Success*
*at the Edge of Your Ability*

### Case Study: Disaster recovery

*Snack attack*

At a leading international food and drink show, one exhibitor's graphics panels had failed to arrive by the morning before the show opened. They were able to courier across several flatpack outer casings for their snacks brand and simply built the boxes on-site and stacked them against the shell scheme to create false walls covered in their branding. A simple, quick and effective solution that almost looked as though it was planned.

A great solution to this would have been to carry a USB with your graphics on with you as part of your Show Survival Pack. A quick call to the organiser's office would be required to obtain the services of a local printer who can have replacement graphics on-site by the build deadline and, hey presto, your pre-planned messaging is still available.

Having spent time thinking about your stand design as part of the planning process, it's likely that you'll be pleased with how it develops on-site and experience few issues with the structural elements. However, it can get stressful during the build and although it might seem that nothing will be ready in time, there's a certain magic about trade shows that sees everything fall into place just before doors open. However, arriving early, being fully prepared and working collaboratively with your team (internal or your agency) will all contribute to ensuring you're back at the hotel enjoying a relaxed dinner while several of your fellow exhibitors are still stressing about missing graphics and finding their stand.

Those last few hours on-site once your stand is fully erected can be vital in ensuring you know how everything works, where everything is and how to get the best out of your kit. Take a walk through your stand from a visitor's perspective – is there a flow that leads them naturally from one section to another in the way you anticipated? If not, how can you tweak it? If you're using any type of technical equipment, sampling or demonstrations, do you know where all the relevant kit is? Is the tech all working and do you know how to reboot it should it fail at any point during the show? Later in this chapter we'll discuss training your stand squad (ideally several weeks before the show), but when your team arrive on the morning of the show you'll want to walk them through the stand with authority as they look to you to gain confidence from your leadership.

As soon as the show opens you'll be busy managing your squad, connecting with visitors and generally running a productive stand, so there's no better time to get a good look at what everyone else is doing than when everyone has set up and gone home (or before they all arrive in the morning). It's a really valuable experience to walk around with a critical eye over other stands thinking about all the decisions you had to make in the planning stages. You'll quickly recognise where someone has too much clutter and barriers or where there are too many words on graphics making it difficult to understand the proposition. You'll also find some inspiration where exhibitors have been creative with a limited budget or delivered massive impact through using new printing or stand design techniques. It's also worth noting if there are any stands that are doing something unusual or quirky – they're likely to be the talk of the show and on occasion can be a great opening line with visitors, asking if they've visited yet or what they thought. While you're walking round it's also worth noting where the nearest toilets/café/cash machine/entrance/live theatre are – you'll be amazed by how many times you're asked that during the course of the show.

The final thing to do before you head back to the hotel and relax before a busy day is secure your stand. Thankfully venues are much better than in previous years at only giving access to registered contractors but, for both build and breakdown, work on the premise that if it can walk, there's a good chance it will. Lock away any portable kit or tech, cover up samples or giveaways (if you don't have room to store them) and don't leave anything valuable to chance. Once you're totally happy with the look of your stand and how it operates then it's time to relax and enjoy the experience of seeing all your hard work convert into high-potential leads.

## 4.2 Selecting your stand squad

In planning exhibitions, we see so many businesses put all their time, effort and resource into designing a stand and choosing their giveaways without giving much thought to who will actually be engaging with visitors. Often, it's a case of whoever is available to come along on the day, although there are usually far more volunteers when the location is Barcelona or Las Vegas than when it's Birmingham! Undoubtedly, choosing who is going to represent your business on the stand and training them before the show are two of the most important elements of executing a successful event. Industry research suggests that 85% of the success of a stand is down to staff, yet

86% of those who work on trade shows have never had any sort of training before they are let loose on visitors. Can you honestly say that in your trade show planning you spend 85% of your time thinking about who is going to be representing your business on the stand and how you give them the best chance of succeeding?

Many exhibitors work on the assumption that by creating a high-impact stand and deploying their best sales staff on the floor they're giving themselves the best possible chance of generating high-quality leads. You would think that the obvious choice would be the front-line sales team as they are more used to the cut and thrust of meeting customers, negotiating prices and closing deals. Those salespeople are successful because they're driven by individual sales targets and rewards and have a contact list full of people they have established relationships with or have time to nurture. Engaging with visitors who may or may not have an interest in your product and quickly filtering whether they are a lucrative prospect requires a very different skillset to those deployed in the field. Often field salespeople can be the least effective people to have on your stand as there is no direct incentive for them. Working to a more corporate agenda that may not have a tangible impact on their own performance (and reward) might not be a great motivator for salespeople making it a challenge to hold their interest in an event.

Thinking of your team as a squad gives you the flexibility to use a range of different skills and experiences, selecting people because of the unique value they can bring to achieving your objectives. Realistically, you might not always have a choice about the type of people you can get to work on your stand, either because you're running your own business where it's just you or because you simply don't have the luxury or choice. However, by understanding some of the different types of characteristics often seen on trade show stands you will better recognise how you can deploy their behaviours for maximum impact (and hide the ones that are less useful!).

## How many do I need?

Starting with the basics, how many people should you have on a stand? It's a great question and one to keep in mind when booking your stand – the more space you have, the more people you need to fill it! It's always best practice to have a minimum of two people regardless of size. Trade shows are exhausting, and you'll need a break – you really aren't going to be able to last all day without going to the loo so who keeps an eye on your stand when nature calls if there's just you – a friendly neighbouring exhibitor? Equally, eating and drinking on your stand never looks good but you will be more effective with some nourishment, so at least with two people you can take a break, wander round, gauge the general vibe of the show and get some fuel.

So if one is too few, how many is too many? We've seen huge corporate stands that have drafted in sales staff, technical experts, customer service and a logistics team to cover every angle a visitor may have. Dressed in corporate uniform they're easily recognisable but quite often can be perceived as a team of bouncers, defensively protecting their stand. Or, because they haven't seen each other for a while they spend most of the show just catching up and chewing the fat with each other. Both situations can be off-putting for visitors who feel as though they're either invading a sacred space or interrupting a team meeting. Industry averages recommend one person per eight square metres of space, with a minimum of two. So if you're booking a 5m × 5m space, giving you 25m altogether you'd be looking for around three or four staff members. These don't necessarily have to be the same people every day – if your business has enough people, bringing in fresh blood every day can really energise your offer and helps everyone learn and build their skills.

## Roles and responsibilities

Establishing clear roles and responsibilities can help each member of your squad understand better how they contribute more effectively to achieving the show's objectives. Without that clarity, it makes it more difficult to filter and channel visitors to the right person to get the best return from their potential.

So what are the different roles and responsibilities on a trade show stand?

- **Project manager:** Hopefully you've picked up this book because you have some direct responsibility for planning and executing your organisation's trade shows. If so, congratulations you've just landed the job of project manager, without doubt the most important job in the squad. The project manager is the go-to person for staff, organisers, stand designers and any other stakeholder who needs information or direction. It's the person who knows inside-out how the stand works, where the spares are stored, which hotels people are staying in and what's happening with leads after the show closes. It's the person who can lay their hands on the risk assessment at a moment's notice when the health and safety officer asks for it or has several copies of the CEO's key note speech on different memory sticks just in case! Ultimately, it's the person with whom the buck stops and depending on the scale and frequency of the trade show campaign it can be an almost full-time job.

- **Stand host:** The person who makes first contact with a visitor, establishes some early rapport and can quickly filter and direct them to the appropriate colleague on the stand. This has to be someone who is comfortable striking up a conversation with customers, can listen more than they can talk and asks the right questions. It's also someone who's not afraid to close down a conversation and dispatch a visitor if there's no prospect of them buying from you. It's also useful to get your stand host to keep a general watching brief over the whole area. It's amazing how quickly stands can get cluttered and untidy and while it's everyone's responsibility to tidy up it never hurts to have someone with a helicopter view. Get the whole team to adopt the Disney approach, no matter what your role is in one of their theme parks or what position it states on their name badge, if they see rubbish or an untidy area they have to stop and rectify the issue.

- **Technical expert:** If you have a complex or specialist product that buyers may have technical questions about having a production expert on hand is crucial. It's the person who can explain how your product works in language that visitors understand and appreciate the problem that your product is trying to solve. Technical experts are passionate about the design of your product and thrive in a situation where they can get into the nitty-gritty of its operations with an appreciative audience – they may not, however, be the best person at stopping visitors and finding out what they need. Additionally, beware if they usually tend to take issue with criticism of 'their' baby as this isn't the time or place for those conversations.

- **Media and PR:** We'll talk more in Chapter 6 about how to maximise your chances of coverage through the visiting media but what's most crucial is consistent messaging. You want the media reporting on your priorities in a way that best inspires your audience but potentially each of your stand staff might have a slightly different interpretation of the message. Allocating the responsibility of media management to one person ensures you can be confident that the narrative being shared is the one you would want.

- **Customer service:** Trade shows are as valuable for engaging with existing customers as they are new, and hopefully lots of the feedback you'll hear is positive and supportive. There may be, however, one or two disgruntled customers who seek you out to have the discussion about late deliveries or faulty goods, so it's worth having someone who's familiar with your policies and procedures and can move the conflict off the stand and deal with it quickly and quietly. On a more positive note, it's great if they can also capture some testimonials from satisfied customers to use in future marketing – a quick vox pop on a camera phone might be all you need.

- **Sales:** Having said that sales might not be your first choice for stand staff, you're probably going to need someone with some sales experience on hand for the definite buyers and interested browsers who are wanting to talk about pricing, promotions and credit accounts. They might not be at their best being deployed front of house meeting and greeting visitors, but they'll be invaluable in sealing the deal with customers who are ready to buy.

- **Data capture:** We'll discuss this more in the next chapter under follow-up, but you might want to assign one squad member overall responsibility for recording data. This isn't necessarily about capturing visitor data, as this should be everyone's responsibility but more general data such as total number of visitors, collecting some testimonials, attendees at theatre presentations, etc.

## Stand staff personas

Not everyone is great at trade shows. There, we've said it!

The often-unspoken truth of trade shows and exhibitions is that somehow, we just expect everyone to be 'good' at them – after all it's just talking to people about what you spend most of your time doing right? Wrong! In case you didn't get it when we've mentioned it before, trade shows are *hard work*! Physically, emotionally, mentally they're draining and for some people it's just about the worst thing you can ask them to get involved in. The simple answer, if someone really doesn't want to do them, don't take them. You're just wasting their time and yours in trying to motivate them and it will show in the way you engage with visitors. So if they're not excited and motivated then leave them in the office.

That doesn't mean to say that everyone who wants to work on your stand is going to be naturally brilliant. Just because someone loves chatting to people all day doesn't mean they're the right person to listen to visitors, understand their problem and offer your product as the solution. But having someone who does want to be there gives you much more to work with than someone who doesn't.

*You'll only have 3–5 minutes on average with a trade show visitor, so you'll need to be sure you have your most engaging and polished people staffing your exhibit. Let your squad know that you are making a big investment to have a presence at the show and that they have been carefully selected based on their superb skill set to ensure that your organisation gets a return on this investment. Set the stage so that you have the right mix of personality types, not to mention a few socially savvy folks that will amplify your presence.* (Campanaro, 2017)

Over the years we've been working in trade shows we've seen a whole host of different stand staff representing businesses but there are some definite 'types' of exhibitor that you can identify. We've identified seven personas of characters we regularly see at trade shows but bear in mind these are exaggerated to make the point, although you can probably identify yourself and some of your colleagues in each of them. Equally, we just liked the alliteration of the character names, but they are equally likely to be from either gender and we've seen as many Freebie Franks and Hard-Sell Hannahs as we have Phoebes and Hanks.

Equally, we're not saying any of these characters are 'good' or 'bad' – there are some traits of each one that will be hugely effective at trade shows, but there are also some traits that don't work quite so well in that environment. What we're trying to give you through these characters is an illustration of some of the behaviours you might recognise and share some inspiration of how you blend and encourage the best in everyone to deliver a great show.

**Freebie Phoebe**

Freebie Phoebe loves trade shows and will usually always be one of the first people to volunteer to attend. She's outgoing, friendly and open but lacks the confidence or knowledge to develop a conversation beyond simply handing out free gifts.

1. **Objective:** To distribute as many pens, caps, notebooks or whatever giveaways you're using as possible.

2. **Opening question:** Would you like one of my free pens?

3. **Follow-up question:** Would you like a free cap as well?

4. **Characteristics:** Happy to stop visitors to make sure they have your giveaway but misses the opportunity to follow up with meaningful questions to understand a visitor's needs. Doesn't think about how the giveaways are being used to help engage visitors with your proposition and drive a brand association.

5. **How to manage:** Could be employed as Stand Host being comfortable in stopping and talking to customers. Developing a set of opening questions to filter visitors and move them over to the right colleague will help them add more value to the stand.

**Jack the Lad**

Jack the Lad loves the opportunity a trade show gives him to visit exotic locations, hang out in the bar and show off his latest bit of designer tech. Jack will know all your fellow exhibitors by the end of the show, have given his phone number out to the most attractive visitors and will have some wild tales to tell about midnight feasts and casino trips.

1. **Objective:** To have fun and meet new people.

2. **Opening line:** Alright fella, is that the old iWatch you're wearing?

3. **Follow-up question:** Do you like mine, it's the newer version?

4. **Characteristics:** Jack will probably arrive most mornings slightly hungover and smelling of stale beer, then spend the first hour telling anyone who will listen about how he was the life and soul of last night's party and how they almost got arrested. By that time, he's recovered enough to sneak off for a bacon sandwich and a coffee, followed by visiting the stands of exhibitors he's personally interested in buying from. His afternoon is usually spent linking up with all his new friends to make arrangements for tonight's party.

5. **How to manage:** Setting standards for your whole team about what's expected and acceptable at the show in the context of what you're trying to achieve can help to set the tone for the entire event. Sharing objectives and planning opening questions might help Jack to focus on why you're there. However, Jack can be useful for his energy at evening network events when the rest of the team are exhausted!

### Wallflower Wilma

Wallflower Wilma will usually avoid working at trade shows and will only do them if she is absolutely forced to. She's shy, lacks confidence and is somewhat of an introvert. The thought of speaking to strangers usually brings her out in cold sweats.

1. **Objective:** To hide at the back of the stand and avoid eye-contact with anyone for the entire duration of the show.

2. **Opening line:** Err, um, ah, hello.

3. **Follow-up question:** Err, um, are you having a good day?

4. **Characteristics:** Very nervous and will find 'jobs' to do on the stand such as tidying and re-arranging to avoid having to speak with anyone. Struggles to start a conversation with visitors and even if she can, keeps the conversation to pleasantries, afraid to move it onto a more commercial establishment of needs.

5. **How to manage:** Leave her in the office if she is genuinely that nervous and doesn't want to be at the event. If Wilma is part of your team, try to understand what's driving her anxiety – is it lack of knowledge or fear of sounding stupid? – and work out a training plan that overcomes this. Give her time to learn more about your products and services and practice, practice, practice starting conversations. Finally, help build her confidence at the show by acknowledging when she's engaging with visitors, send her on errands to speak to friendly exhibitors you know to give her confidence in asking questions and listening.

**Chatty Charlie**

Chatty Charlie likes nothing more than meeting new people, finding out all about them and what's happening in their world. Charlie makes friends wherever he goes, and people often know more about him than they ever wanted to within five minutes of meeting him. TV, sport, weather, religion, food, politics, health, holidays – there's no subject that Charlie isn't keen to let you know his opinion on.

1.  **Objective:** To talk to everyone about everything.

2. **Opening line:** So where have you come from today?

3. **Follow-up question:** We went there once, back in 2007 I think, no 2008, we took the A1 so we could see the scenery, stopped off at this little café in the hills, served gorgeous cakes and the owners told about this pub that was just a short detour into the village that brewed its own beer, so once we'd finished our cakes… (and on and on and on).

4. **Characteristics:** Charlie is always talking to someone, whether it's a visitor, an exhibitor, a stand-builder or a cleaner – it doesn't matter who his audience is he just likes telling them stories about his life. Listening to other people is just a pause for breath for Charlie as he thinks about the next topic he's going to tell people about. Charlie does ask questions but it's usually about their life and family rather than business, and only ever as an excuse to give him some thinking time.

5. **How to manage:** Squad training should reinforce to Charlie that you're attending the show for a specific reason and because you're trying to achieve SMART business objectives. Walking through the stand design, opening questions and script for conversations might help Charlie appreciate he needs to be more commercial in his conversations. Busy stands attract other visitors as we're naturally quite nosey, so if it's quiet, Charlie is great in getting conversations going that attract other visitors over to your stand.

**Supermodel Selena**

Supermodel Selena always looks polished, professional and slightly aloof. Her ability to last all day in skyscraper heels is the envy of the trade show and her perfectly manicured nails obviously haven't been involved in ripping open boxes and building stands. Selena will need a ten-minute break every hour to visit the ladies and ensure every hair is in place and her lipstick hasn't smudged. Most of the time she can remember the name of the company she's working for but that's not always guaranteed.

1. **Objective:** To look good.

2. **Opening line:** Good morning, what line of business are you in sir?

3. **Follow-up question:** That sounds very interesting.

4. **Characteristics:** Selena will be the smartest looking person on your stand and will be horrified if you try and make her wear a baggy, bobbly polo shirt. Her professional appearance will give your stand a perception of quality and attract visitors who are interested in a more in-depth discussion about your product or service. However, Selena can be more interested in her appearance than your product and lack substance when asked to answer more detailed or technical questions.

5. **How to manage:** As with other characters, Selena will benefit from clear training about the objectives for the show along with concise details about the product features and benefits to build her knowledge. Selena can be an impressive stand host when prepped on the most effective opening questions and can attract and filter visitors before referring them to the most appropriate colleague on the stand.

**Hard-sell Hank**

Hard-sell Hank might well be the best salesman you have in the field, very competitive and driven by pursuing high-value sales to generate a juicy bonus. Hard-sell Hank will always be closing the deal from the first hello and isn't interested in small-talk or finding out about what a customer's specific needs are, he's just convinced that whatever he's selling is the answer to their prayers.

1. **Objective:** To sell… lots.

2. **Opening line:** So how many would you like?

3. **Follow-up question:** And how will you be paying for that – cash, card, on account?

4. **Characteristics:** Undoubtedly Hank can sell, but it may not always be to willing customers and this could lead to challenges for the customer service team if you offer a cooling off period following the show. Hank is agitated if he's not selling, easily bored and thinking about all the sales he could be making out in the field to beat his individual target. Hank is a broadcaster, talking at people about the features of your product or service, failing to link them to any tangible benefit for the customer and hardly, if at all, listening to their actual needs. Hank can easily become disgruntled and even rude if he feels others on the stand are performing better than he is.

5. **How to manage:** Hank might struggle in an environment where he's working towards a corporate goal rather than his own individual targets, or where he's not directly selling. Setting incentives and daily competitions based on your overall objectives will help fuel his competitive nature. At your team's training, helping Hank to understand the product features and benefits, and the opportunity to match these to a customer's needs, might help rein in his inner salesman – especially if he's able to listen and use a customer's responses to up-sell to a higher value item.

**Promiser Pete**

Promiser Pete wants to be everyone's friend and just loves saying yes – to everything! Pete believes the ultimate in customer service is giving a customer everything they ever ask for regardless of whether it's appropriate, relevant or even cost-effective.

1. **Objective:** To get everyone to like him.

2. **Opening line:** Hi, what could we do to help you decide to buy our product?

3. **Follow-up question:** A 50% discount, an all-expenses paid trip to our production facility in Florence and a sale or return basis for an order value of £50 – of course, no problem – nice negotiating with you!

4. **Characteristics:** Promiser Pete is quite often not the most junior member of the team and might not get to meet with customers very regularly. Therefore, he doesn't have the background history on which customers try it on, which customers have real volume potential and what is the 'art of the possible'. New and existing customers may be flattered by meeting a senior member of the team and therefore to save face Pete is happy to agree to all their demands, presuming they are all perfectly possible and leaving the carnage with his team to sort out once he's safely back in the comfort of his glass-walled office.

5. **How to manage:** Senior management can be among the hardest people to brief for a trade show. Undoubtedly their presence adds credibility and many of your customers will expect to see them on-site. Training them separately on the SMART objectives for the show, the parameters the squad is working to and the roles and responsibilities of the team should help them stay on script. Also giving them the heads-up on any potential flash points with customers gives them chance to prepare an appropriate defensive response. If your Promiser Pete is a more junior member of the team who lacks the confidence to say no, again sharing the objectives and parameters for the show should help them prepare their responses to the likely questions along with having a more commercially experienced colleague they can pass visitors over to.

**Unsociable Sam**

Unsociable Sam is the answer to your prayers on all things digital. She'll whip your online profile into shape, share countless pics of your stand on social media and ensure you're part of the wider conversation – but all from behind the safety of a screen and her ear buds. Her dexterity in balancing tablet, phone, camera and earphones is admirable, but ask her to actually have a 'conversation' with a visitor and she'll soon be buried in an urgent re-tweet or Instagram post.

1. **Objective:** To generate as many likes, re-tweets and shares as possible – and avoid all human contact.

2. **Opening line:** Erm, I'm just going to hand you over to my colleague while I take a quick snap for Instagram.

3. **Follow-up question:** Could you just move a bit to the left, so I can see our logo please?

4. **Characteristics:** Unsociable Sam can add real value to your trade show execution by amplifying your presence using digital and social media but she's far more comfortable with conversations on screen than with real people. Sam's knowledge about the different platforms is immense but there's danger that in trying to connect with every possible audience you miss engaging with your most important one. Equally, it can sometimes be difficult to keep Sam on a corporate agenda as opposed to a personal self-gratifying one.

5. **How to manage:** It's helpful to think through the importance of social media and digital to your objectives and your audience before the show – if you're working in a high-tech environment where the audience will be expecting high-quality digital engagement then Sam's earned her place on your squad. However, if it's a more traditional audience where digital engagement is likely to be low, it may be more beneficial for Sam to give the rest of the squad some top tips to execute themselves on-site but leave her in the office for the show. Whether your digital contribution is through Sam (on-site or monitoring things from the office) or your on-site team, it's worth sharing in your training the engagement plan, so your message is consistent and relevant.

*Start your exhibit staff training early and repeat often. Mentally, your squad needs to be well-trained on best practices in face-to-face selling techniques in order to win over your audience. You also need to ensure that they all understand the key messages you need to be conveyed to the visitors, and how the exhibit experience and in-stand technology has been designed to help them convey these messages. It's also important that your squad training includes role play re their interactions with a stand attendee, so they can all deliver your messages confidently, accurately, consistently and concisely.*
(Campanaro, 2017)

*The element of teamwork is perhaps underappreciated.*
—Stewart Butterfield, co-founder of Flickr and Boss at
Slack Technologies, Inc.

Hopefully reading through the different personas you will have recognised some of the people within your own business, or even some of those characteristics in yourself. As we've stated, these are extremes to make the point and there will be several other characters you'll come across as you navigate your trade show journey, but the key is remembering you have the right to select your squad to give you the best chance of success.

One of the main benefits of being able to identify different characters within your team is that it creates the opportunity to blend your team, ensuring you get a good mix of people that can fulfil the different roles rather than a squad of squabbling Hard-sell Hanks! An 'ideal' trade show squad member would exhibit some of the more positive behaviours of each of the personas we've presented.

There are some characters who suit some roles better than other so here are some suggestions about how you might deploy your team if you've a choice of different personalities:

| Stand host | Technical expert | Media and PR | Customer service | Sales |
|---|---|---|---|---|
| Supermodel Selena | Wallflower Wilma | Unsociable Sam | Chatty Charlie | Hard-Sell Hank |
| Freebie Phoebe | | Promiser Pete | Jack the Lad | |
| Jack the Lad | | | | |

It's great to be able to balance your squad but what if you're a micro business owner and you've only got yourself and your mum available to staff your stand? Great work on recruiting your mum, at least you get a coffee and toilet break now while leaving your stand in capable hands. Seriously, if it is only the two of you, there's still the opportunity to reflect on your personalities, strengths and where you might be missing some skills. With all the preparation you have put in to ensuring your proposition and execution is engaging and relevant for customers you can be confident in bringing out your inner Charlie or Hank, as you know your product or service will be of interest to visitors. If you're naturally a Hank or a Charlie, revisit your commercial proposition, be clear how your product or service solves a problem for your audience and make that the starting point for any conversation with a visitor remembering to listen to what they actually need and not want you think they want.

We'll talk about squad training shortly, but in recognising the characters within your team you have the opportunity for them to support each other and build your organisational capability – the whole process of trade shows can be a learning opportunity for everyone. For example, can Hard-Sell Hank work with Chatty Charlie to help Charlie gain the skills to get to the commercial conversation more quickly. Equally, can Hard-Sell Hank understand the benefits of investing in conversation with a customer through learning from Charlie? Jack the Lad might be able to help Wilma build her confidence, by sharing anecdotes about how he just starts conversations with people he's never met. This transfer of knowledge and skills has the potential to enhance your business long after the show has closed and helps your team understand the dynamics of the squad and how they can benefit from each other back in their day jobs.

*Fifty-seven per cent of exhibitors said that their trade show staff gained sales skills from exhibiting. Other skills gained were summarised as: product knowledge (46%) and staff bonding (38%).*
(Display Wizard, 2018)

### 4.3 Opening lines

Which leads us nicely onto how you start a conversation with a visitor at a trade show. Not something you might have thought of as important when planning for a trade show but unquestionably one of the most crucial parts of pre-planning for yourself and your squad. Often exhibitors spend thousands of pounds investing in a trade show but forget to spend half an hour thinking about the first words they utter to a visitor that could make or break the relationship with a potentially valuable customer.

Before we go any further, think about the last trade show you exhibited at; what was the first thing you said to visitors as they passed by your stand? Was it the same for every customer or did it vary depending on whether they looked vaguely interested or whether they were marching past, obviously on their way somewhere else?

Now think about the last trade show you attended as a visitor and how exhibitors greeted you as you passed, what was your response? How did you react to their questions and were there some opening lines that engaged with you more quickly than others?

Here are some of the favourite opening lines used by hundreds, if not thousands of exhibitors across the globe:

- Hi, how's your day going?
- Hi, how are you?
- Hi, are you enjoying the show?
- Hi, have your heard about our latest product/service?
- Hi, would you like a sample/pen/freebie?
- Hi, have you found what you're looking for today?

The most likely answer to all these closed questions is either yes, no or fine. They give the visitor every chance to escape quickly and quietly without even starting to establish whether what you have to offer is of any value in solving their problem. But they are the questions that get used most frequently when trying to initiate a conversation with a visitor and often generate a look of wonderment from those uttering the words as the potential customer saunters off to another stand.

So, here are a few things to think about when forming your opening questions:

- **Keep it open:** Use questions that start with *what, why, how* or *tell me about*, and encourage the visitor to go into more detail about their opinions, feelings and needs. Questions such as 'How are you today?' may seem professional and polite but are an open invitation for visitors to respond with an equally polite 'Great thanks' and keep moving on.

- **Questions you care about the answer to:** Do you really care how someone feels or are you more interested in finding out whether your product or service could be of use to them? You'll likely come across as more engaging and genuinely interested in listening to their response if it matters to you.

- **Ground it in their needs:** Ensure the question is more about why they're visiting or what they're looking for, rather than asking for permission to tell them how brilliant your product is. For example, 'What are you looking for from today's show?' rather than 'Can I have five minutes to take you through the latest version of our widget?'

- **Make it relatable to your objectives:** Remember all that hard work that went into setting your objectives? Now's the time it's really useful in ensuring that the opening lines you use start to navigate whether a random visitor has the potential to buy from you. What are you trying to achieve and how can you start a dialogue that guides you towards that from the very first interaction?

- **Understand the 'path to purchase':** Think about how a visitor might respond to your question (and there might be several different responses) and where you will need to go next to start filtering whether you have any common ground for doing business. Try not to use questions where you will find it difficult to deal with the response, e.g., 'Have you enjoyed using our product in the past?' opens up the opportunity for a visitor to tell you how much they hate your product (although that's valuable feedback and it's certainly filtering non-buyers out!).

Plotting your opening lines and path to purchase can be a significant help to your squad in several ways. Although you don't all want to come across as robots repeating the same line, having a consistent approach should help to keep everyone focused on your SMART objectives and reinforce their role in the team. You might want to have a few different options planned so that waiting visitors aren't overhearing the same generic greeting from your whole squad. However, don't be afraid to change things if they're not working. It's great to have a plan but if on-site you're not getting the response you anticipated from visitors, listen to your team and take their feedback on how to adapt your opening (for more on daily wash-ups see below).

A good case study on mixing questions up can be taken from how McDonald's trained their staff when they first opened franchises in the UK. They had four opening greetings and four closing statements. They reasoned that the person fourth in line couldn't hear the first greeting but would subsequently hear the second, third and fourth one so when they were greeted by the first one, as they got to the front of the queue, they thought they were getting a personised greeting and an individual thank you statement which made them feel valued. By mixing your greetings and farewells up between your squad it is likely that your visitors will feel welcomed and more inclined to engage with them as they will be seen to be giving individual attention to all their visitors.

Quite often something might emerge on-site that helps you start conversations quite naturally, for example at one show there was a fantastic new coffee roaster who was offering samples of steaming hot, strong coffee in branded cups that everyone seemed to be carrying and talking about. This created a natural opening line for an exhibitor to comment 'Oh I see you've got one of those great cups of coffee – was that something you were particularly interested in finding at today's show?' which opened up the opportunity for a visitor to share their interests and reasons for visiting, which in turn helps with the initial visitor filtering process. If you see a visitor carrying literature from another stand offering a similar product to yours or notes from a speaker session relating to your industry, it gives you another clue that they might be interested in your offer. This creates an opportunity for a personalised opening line by enquiring what they thought of the live session or how the competitor's product was able to solve a potential issue for them.

Equally, for those members of your squad who are anxious about starting conversations with visitors, having a range of planned openings that they can rehearse before even getting on-site could help them feel more relaxed and able to engage with more people with confidence. It's worth reminding your team that they might not be the only ones nervous of starting a conversation as not every visitor is going to be a natural extrovert. So, if you ask a closed question and get a short, curt response it might be just as much to do with the shyness of the visitor as your questioning technique. Whatever you can do to put people at ease and make them forget they're actually in a sales environment, the more mutually beneficial your conversations are likely to be.

The right opening line will depend on your specific circumstance and objectives but here are a few suggestions to get you thinking about your own:

- What was the reason you decided to visit the show today?

- What's been the most exciting thing you've seen at the show so far today? (Although this can put people on the spot and make them feel a little uncomfortable.)

- Tell me about how you're hoping your organisation will benefit from visiting today's show?

- What part of our industry is your business involved in?

- Tell me about the challenges that you're hoping to find a solution for today?

- How useful do you find this show compared to others you've visited?

- What's caught your eye during your tour of the show today?

These sorts of questions might be quite different from those visitors hear repeated on other stands so immediately you'll come across as more invested and engaging than the robots who just asked how their day was!

And to see how the experts do it (or don't do) there's a great video from Spark Media Solutions at the 'Trade Show for Trade Show People' which demonstrates brilliantly why it's not as easy as it might seem… even for those employed in the exhibition industry; www.youtube.com/watch?v=cV3MUxn02NU.

Of course, there's always the option to ditch the questions altogether and let your stand do the talking for you. There are a whole host of gimmicks and techniques that exhibitors have used over the years to grab the attention of visitors from live demonstrations, to celebrities, to interactive games and magic curtains. These are all brilliant ways to capture the attention and disrupt a visitor from a seemingly endless row of non-descript booths. Two notes of caution, however, on relevance and follow-up. Attention-grabbers work particularly well when they are relevant to your audience and show how your product meets their need, leading onto a naturally evolved conversation.

A great example of how to grab people's attention was used by Charity Water. They create safe water supplies for remote villages around the world whose residents regularly walk two to three miles a day carrying 80lbs of water. To connect with visitors, they challenged them to walk 50 yards up and down a ramped platform carrying 40lbs of water in two containers. The flooring was adorned with messages about how many school days children had lost carrying water to their villages each year and how their work changed people's lives for the better. The experience created was designed to both inspire and educate the participants and onlookers alike to act, e.g., donate.

The technique you use should be memorable in a way that reminds a visitor who you are and why you're important to them. Even after the theatre of the attention-grabber, a prospect is going to want to speak with one of your squad about the details, so it's just as important to understand how to navigate the conversation after you've caught their eye. Your attention-grabber is likely to attract some of the 80% of visitors who aren't in a position to buy from you, so it's equally important to be able to follow-up to filter out those who are less valuable.

Opening lines are the real moment of truth for visitors, the time when all the planning, the pre-show marketing and the last-minute nerves come together in the opportunity to actually speak with a potential buyer. All the hard work, stress and investment has the potential to come to nothing if you can't engage with visitors in a way that's meaningful for both parties, resulting in spending too much time with people who will never buy your product, or too little time with those who might. It's one of the elements that so often gets left out of the planning process but has the potential to make a massive impact on the success of an entire event.

## 4.4 Squad training

*Ants are successful creatures: they are successful because they know very well that the mind of the team is superior to the mind of the individual.*

—Mehmet Murat ildan, Turkish playwright, novelist and thinker

Selecting your squad and thinking through how you're going to engage with visitors is a great start to ensuring that all your hard work and plans convert into profitable leads. However, if you don't share your strategy with your squad and help them understand what you're trying to achieve it can all be for nothing. You might think that your stand design and giveaways are going to be the most influential elements in drawing visitors to talk to you, but as we've stated previously, 85% of the success of your stand will be down to how your staff present themselves and behave. Bearing that in mind, surely, it's worth investing some time and effort into ensuring you're giving your squad everything they need to do the best job they can – but surprisingly, only 26% of exhibitors conduct any training for all or most events, 50% rarely hold any training for their staff leaving a further 24% with no training at all according to a 2012 Centre for Exhibition Industry Research (CEIR) report (Adams, 2012).

How, where and when you train your squad will depend on several variables including the scale of the show, size of your team, previous experience, complexity of the stand, availability and geography. Ideally you would want to be training your squad collectively around four weeks ahead of the show. This creates the opportunity for your squad to bond, understand each other's roles and work out where they might be able to support each other. Although you might need to take time out to deliver a training session, it will inevitably be more efficient than trying to train each member of the team individually. By training your team ahead of time you're supporting them to absorb the information, familiarise themselves with how the stand works, understand their role on it and even make suggestions about how things could still be improved before the show opens. Even if there are only two of you attending an event, it's still worth taking a couple of hours to talk through the plans and responsibilities to ensure that you're both fully aligned on what's expected of each other. Modern tech also enables remote training using video conferencing if it's impossible to get everyone together in the same room, but as trade shows are all about face-to-face engagement, there's nothing like setting the tone right from the start. If you feel that you lack the skills internally to deliver the right level of training to achieve the right outcomes, then source a good provider who can.

Before you get too far into the detail of the five elements that make a comprehensive training session, it's worth acknowledging with your squad that trade shows are hard work, physically, emotionally and mentally (there may just be a few weaker members of the squad who self-deselect at this point if it sounds too much like hard work) and how much the business appreciates their efforts in this endeavour.

These five key elements should form the core of your training, ensuring that your squad have everything they need to maximise all the effort you have put in so far:

1. **SMART objectives:** We've mentioned that, especially for sales people, it can be difficult to get excited about trade shows when staff can't see a direct impact on their job or targets. Sharing how trade shows form part of an aligned marketing plan and where they fit in to delivering an overall corporate agenda can help your squad to see the relevance and understand the investment (which can often be perceived as a waste of money by some unenlightened staff members). It's a great opportunity to remind your team of the bigger corporate vision, update them on your current business performance (compare yourself to where you feel you stand in relation to your competition as well at this point) and refresh them on the image that the business wants to project to the industry. Drilling down into the SMART objectives for the show itself and illustrating what good looks like will help your squad understand what is expected of them and how they can contribute to the overall results. For example, if your aim is to recruit five high potential contacts and you have five members of staff, it can be reassuring for them to hear that you're only expecting each person to find one great contact – this feels much more manageable than saying 'we're here to meet loads of new people'. It also means you're more

likely to ensure the leads you generate have real potential as opposed to collecting random contacts in a race to the biggest number.

2. **Stand induction:** You've put your heart and soul into designing a stand which you're confident delivers relevance, engagement and excitement for your visitors, but you'll soon find everyone on your team is a critic and can't wait to tell you how you should have done it differently. There's nothing more disheartening when you're bursting with excitement on day one for your squad to arrive (usually late), suck in their cheeks and say 'Wouldn't have used that strapline'. Taking the time to share your thinking with the squad, explaining why you have designed the stand in a particular way and more importantly why that matters to a visitor can help to prevent some of those conversations. Your squad might still not agree with every design decision, but if you can prove you made it based on logic it becomes more difficult for them to argue with and easier to get them to buy into your thinking. This is also the time to share with your squad exactly how the stand works, how visitors will navigate it, how any demonstrations or sampling activity will work, what the giveaways and literature are and all the intricacies of how the stand works so they're familiar with it once they get on-site. If you're using a pop-up display, have it ready to show your team at the training session or if you're using a design agency get them to send you a 3D fly-through you can walk your team through in the training (most agencies shouldn't charge for this). This is also the time to share product briefings, cheat sheets, details on show deals, elevator pitches and any other supporting material that will be useful to your team in preparation

for engaging with visitors. Again, this is a great time to pressure test your stand plan with other people, there might be a blind spot you haven't noticed or a flaw in the plan that sharing with fresh eyes reveals while you've still got time to do something about it. A full belt and braces training session would be take the squad away to your stand-builder's premises and have the stand set up for them to physically walk through to take them away from their daily distractions. This of course isn't always possible or practical, but removing the daily grind from their minds will help them focus, so a natural space of any sort would be good.

3. **Stand standards:** This is not one to leave to chance and assume that everyone will have the same perception as you for what is and isn't acceptable on a stand. Quite often this can be something project managers struggle with, especially if they're briefing more senior colleagues. It's worth remembering the level of investment that has gone into getting the project this far, and that it's the role of everyone on the stand to project a professional perception. Working on a trade show stand is neither a right nor a jolly, it's hard work and doing it well requires following a few (common sense) rules in the same way that any other business task would do. The standards you want to set for your stand will depend on what's appropriate for your circumstances, but the most important thing is to set some, brief them and stick to them.

### Great stand management standards

You will need to set the stand rules that are right for you but listed below are some of the commonly agreed elements that ensure you present a professional, friendly and engaging impression.

- **Eating and drinking:** It never looks good when you're talking to a visitor and spraying them with a half-eaten sandwich! The rule should apply to everyone and for everything (including chewing gum and coffee), so make sure you've enough staff to give them a break where they can refuel well away from the stand. This becomes harder if you're offering food and drink as part of your stand design, so just work out what you're happy with your team participating in and set the standards for how you're all going to interact. They need to understand that the temptation to partake in passing sampling opportunities presented by sales staff from other suppliers has to be declined politely and that they can always taste these delights during their designated breaks.

- **Mobile devices:** An increasingly difficult element to manage as we all become more digitally engaged, especially if you're asking people to use social media as part of your marketing. However, there's a difference between someone sending a quick tweet and replying to emails on a laptop or engaging in a call. This just screams to a visitor that you're not really interested in them and have more important things to do. Again, this rule applies to everyone regardless of seniority or role. If they're on the stand, they're there to work the stand. Mobiles should be set to silent and should be checked off the stand if needs be, assuming that there are enough bodies to cover the stand and this activity is strictly managed.

- **Dress code:** Again this will depend on your industry and the expectations the audience will have of how you should dress. A good rule of thumb is to dress as most of your visitors would dress. Uniform is a great option if you want to use your corporate identity to drive awareness and promote a team approach – it's also a great way for visitors to quickly identify who your team are. But beware of black shirts... you can end up looking like nightclub bouncers. If you have a strong character association to your brand you can bring this to life in your dress code, e.g., a fresh produce supplier who wants to bring out the authentic farm experience might dress in wellies, a Barbour waistcoat and flat cap, etc., but make sure it's relevant, obvious and not forced. And for the avoidance of doubt, the days of models (male or female) in skin-tight Lycra are long gone – over-sexualised dress is not appropriate for the majority of mainstream shows. The best piece of advice you can give your team on dress is to be smart and comfortable, especially as regards shoes (but not flip-flops unless that's what you're selling). We often advise to keep an 'Emergency Box' in the storage area with hair brushes, lip balm, plasters, deodorant, water, wipes, painkillers, mints, etc., so if anyone did fall out of bed and onto the stand, at least they could have a quick spray and brush-up before meeting visitors.

- **Conduct:** You've selected your team because they're a great squad of open, friendly, approachable professionals, but it's still worth reminding them what you expect in terms of behaviour. For example, it's not a holiday so don't turn up late and hungover, decide how you will refer to your competition (do not allow the squad to 'bad mouth' your competition as this will be seen as a negative by potential buyers), don't ignore visitors to chat to each other, etc. Establishing your standards and training them ensures that everyone knows what to expect and it's easier to discuss it on-site if people aren't keeping up the team standards. Make it clear how much the company has invested and the professional image you want to portray and their role in that i.e., acting as Jack the Lad at the nightly networking opportunities and then rolling up at the stand smelling of the night before will not only be frowned upon but may have other negative knock-on effects for them going forward.

4. **Filtering visitors:** We'll talk more in the next section about how to filter visitors and identify prospects, but your squad training gives you the perfect opportunity to help your team understand what their specific role in the process is, how to ask the right questions and ensure you're spending the most time with the most valuable prospects. During your training, talk about who your ideal target visitor is, VIPs and media contacts you have invited and the types of visitors to move on. Training like this can create a safe and supportive environment for more nervous members

of your squad to try out some opening lines and role play so they become more familiar with opening and managing conversations with visitors. From experience working with different teams in different industries, role playing while extremely beneficial for some can be daunting, excruciating and extremely embarrassing if done in-house with colleagues no matter how good the facilitator is. If you feel that this type of training would be worth the effort, then we would advocate that you bring in an external resource to both manage this and act as visitors/prospects, so colleagues are not put under undue pressure to act out of character and 'perform'. The safer you can make this training environment feel for individuals and their feelings the better the achievable results will be in the long run (and money well spent!).

5.  **Logistics:** Often this can be the aspect that most of your squad will be interested in – how are they getting there, where are they eating and sleeping and when can they go home? Detailed logistics planning can help save you time in future if you can give everyone every bit of information they need in relation to getting there, getting on-site and getting home again. Key areas to include in the logistics section of your training include badges and registration, transport and car parking, dates and venue, accommodation, evening and networking events and rotas. In addition, it's worth advising your team how much storage space you have on the stand – often people turn up with laptop bags and cases that clutter up the stand and create barriers for visitors. If they've checked out of the hotel, advise them they need to check their bags in with the designated on-site cloakroom, if available, if not they may need to leave their bags at the

hotel and retrieve them afterwards. Producing a pack with hard copies of all the relevant details for each member of the squad can be time-consuming but avoids a million phone calls over the following weeks asking about hotels and dates!

The above should clearly illustrate just how much there is to take your squad through to align them to all the fantastic planning you have been doing over the several months previously. Some will undoubtedly welcome the support and advice and soak it in, others may be trade show veterans and think they have nothing more to learn (the old dogs and new tricks scenario!). The reality is every show will be different even if your company has been doing it for years, and your objectives may change so it's useful to get everyone along to ensure the whole team is working from the same plan. It may be that the company has been doing the show for years, but has it always paid off or has 'routine fatigue' set in? A gentler way of getting those more experienced members of the team, who don't feel they need any training to engage is telling them how much the newer members of the team would benefit from their wisdom, it usually does the trick and they actually learn something new in the process.

We will talk in the next chapter about evaluating show success, which includes on-site briefings, but it's also worth mentioning here that while your main training will be off-site ahead of the show, daily on-site briefings with your team are incredibly useful. Using the www.ebi (what went well – even better if) and T4T (tweaks for tomorrow) methods you can review how things are working on-site, if anything needs changing, where you're having particular success and how your team are performing in their roles to make sure you're using your time at the show as effectively as possible.

Like everything else we've been discussing, squad training takes time and commitment from everyone, but it is after all your people that visitors will be engaging with. It's not all about your graphics or your giveaways, so surely it is worth investing the time in the core element of your stand that has the potential to make the biggest difference?

## 4.5 Filtering visitors – prioritising prospects and leads

You've spent months planning your perfect stand, training your team and inviting your key contacts and now comes the moment of truth when the doors open and a wave of excited, curious potential customers come flooding your way ready to buy. In reality, it can seem somewhat of an anti-climax and often there is more of a trickle than a flood once the doors open, especially if you're towards the back of the show floor where it can take up to an hour for visitors to make their way up to you. However, don't be disheartened, this can be a great time to complete your final checks to ensure that the stand is looking as good as it possibly can, that your squad have had chance to ask all the questions they need to and for you all to take a breath before it gets busy.

However, once those visitors make it towards your section of the hall, it's good to make sure your squad is ready to pounce and convert every passer-by into a potential customer, right? Well no, not quite.

*Research conducted by CEIR suggests that on average between 16% and 20% of all visitors to a trade show will be potential buyers of your product or service.*

If that number sounds low and you're disappointed that only around a fifth of an audience could result in high-quality leads, think of it this way:

- There are four of you on the exhibition stand, with the assumption one person will be on a break rotation most of the time, leaving three people in play to speak to visitors.

- The event organisers have suggested that pre-registrations for the event are around 6,500 people over two days – approximately 3,250 per day.

- Assume 60% of pre-registered visitors attend, that's 1,950 people per day (statistics from the Event Tribe forum suggest a 40–50% dropout rate for pre-registered attendees for free events dependent on several factors, including the weather, compared to an industry average of only a 9% attrition rate for paid-for events).

- That leaves almost 400 people per day who are serious potential buyers of your product or service – or 100 people for each member of your team to engage with.

- If the show is open 10–4 that's 16 people per hour, or one every four minutes – if you don't take a toilet or lunch break.

- And that doesn't include all the tyre-kickers, opera singers, suppliers, media and existing customers (see definitions of visitors below) who are going to be coming your way during the show.

In short, 16–20% of a total visitor audience being able to buy your product should be plenty to identify, engage, follow-up and sell to in order to get a return on your investment.

So how do you filter through the time-wasters and get to those juicy hot leads that are going to justify your investment and set your business on the road to record-breaking sales? Well, the first point to emphasise is that every visitor is valuable to you even if you don't realise it at first. Sure, not every visitor may be in a position to buy, but even those tyre-kickers (see below) who just want your free pen and a chat help your team build their skills in politely and professionally dispatching time-wasters (not in the sense of a Mafia hitman scoping your unwanted targets from the rafters!). Equally, you never know who they know that might be a useful contact, or whether in a year or two's time they have moved up the ranks and have become a potential buyer of your offerings. The behaviour of everyone on your stand towards visitors, regardless of their 'usefulness' to you at this point in time reflects your brand and business so everyone deserves respect and courtesy *at all times*!

We'll shortly talk about some of the characters you might come across during a trade show so that you can easily identify them, but as a starting point it's useful to think about how you will categorise visitors once you've engaged with them. Visitors will probably fall into four main categories:

- **Passers-by:** Those visitors with whom you've had a nice chat but there is no potential for any mutual business and no reason to keep in touch – you cannot add value to each other's business in any way.

- **Contact:** Someone who may be useful in future but who is unlikely to be an immediate sales prospect. This may be the media, a supplier, someone who wants to collaborate or someone who is thinking about possibly starting a business that might use your services.

- **Prospect:** Someone who has expressed an interest in your product or service but who is not in a position to buy right now, either because they're not the decision-maker or the decision will not be taken until sometime in the future. These visitors are key to filling your sales pipeline and it's crucial to keep in touch with them, adding value with useful information or advice over the coming months until they become a more serious lead. They may have become a lead by the time you exhibit at you next show.

- **Lead:** Someone who has visited the show with the intention of finding solutions to problems and buying at some point in the near future. These visitors are like gold dust and there may only be three or four at a show but they are in a very strong position to buy and are looking for the final pieces of the jigsaw to complete the transaction. The key action with these visitors is to ensure there is a clear follow-up action in the diary such as a meeting or date to submit a proposal. A visitor only becomes a lead when a clear follow-up action (e.g., meeting, adding to a newsletter circulation, follow-up literature) has been agreed with a specific reason to keep in touch.

It can be difficult at first contact to tell which category visitors fall into, especially if they take control of the conversation, but some clever probing and questioning will help lead them through a series of disclosures to a point where your team can identify which category they fall into (that, and some easy-to-spot buying signals – see below).

*Sixty-four per cent of trade show visitors are not customers of the business stand they visited – Source: Exhibitor Survey Inc.*
(*XL Displays, 2017*)

**How do you decipher buying signals at a trade show?**

- **Affirmative gestures** such as head-nodding, verbal agreements, leaning forward, positive reinforcement of points you're making all show they're following the logic of your argument.

- **Asking questions** about how your product or service works – especially the technicalities, this shows they're thinking about how it applies to their businesses.

- **Seeking logistical details** such as price, delivery, lead times, promotional support, etc. all show they have moved beyond just being interested in what your product or service has to offer.

- **Demonstrations:** asking to see how the product works, understand different models and amendments, thinking through which version of your product might be best suited for them.

- **Touch, feel, smell, taste:** hopefully only the last one if you're a food producer, but if they're looking to get hold of your product and inspect it close up and personal, they're interested! Taste is difficult at trade shows as everyone expects samples even if they're not a potential buyer such as a food store owner, but remember everyone is a potential consumer and even if they can't buy directly from you, you do want them to pick it up next time they see it in their local store and to share their experience with others.

- **Repetition:** if you find yourself covering points you've already addressed this is a good sign as a buyer is looking for clarification on a few outstanding matters before making a final decision. Equally, if a customer repeats a benefit you've articulated your product will deliver it shows they have noticed/listened to what you have said and are thinking about it in the context of their own business and the benefits it can bring them.

- **Reading:** if they turn to your literature and start studying it, don't panic that you've lost them, they're just looking for more evidence that they're making the right decision. If you get a sense of what might help them decide, i.e., advocacy, you can point them to customer testimonials that might influence them. However, if it's not clear exactly what they're looking for then give them the space to find the answer for themselves. If they look puzzled after reading the literature ask if they have found what they were looking for and signpost them to the information.

- **Comparison:** if a visitor states they've tried a competitor version previously and can comment how yours is a better alternative it's a strong signal they're in a positive mood to buy.

- **Anxiety:** if prospects are about to make a buying decision, or commit to a next meeting they might look a little nervous, start touching their face, looking to their fellow visitors, etc. Try to put them at their ease and ask them if there is anything else they're concerned about that you can help with. They're about to invest in an unknown entity, even if it's just their time for a meeting so it's only expected that they might be a bit anxious.

- **Enthusiasm:** the easiest buying signal to spot, they talk eagerly about how they see your product or service fitting into their business, mention being excited by talking about it their colleagues and generally show interest and eagerness to get their hands on their purchase.

- **Next steps:** when a visitor starts to ask about next steps and actions, this is a clear signal they're open to a further discussion and want to learn more about you in a more formal environment.

### Tell-tale signs that a visitor isn't interested in your proposition

- **Non-responsive:** If a visitor doesn't respond to your friendly approach or just smiles and walks straight past they have already de-selected themselves from being a potential buyer of your product. Equally, if you ask them about the problems they currently have in their business and it draws a blank it shows they're not really in solutions mode, or they don't understand what the problem is at the moment, so avoid making them feel uncomfortable and politely move them on.

- **Price:** If they ask about price before anything else they're probably not going to buy. They're not interested in the benefits of your product or service or how it fits into their organisation, but they can justify that they've ruled it out based on budget constraints – they haven't, they're just not interested, and this is their 'get out'.

- **Time limits:** If they answer your opening question with 'OK, but I've only got a minute' they're probably not that interested in what you have to say and are just being polite. You do still have an opportunity to wow them and influence their opinion, but they don't have time for answering questions, so this will have to be more of a 'tell' about what you do in the hope that you land on a problem that you can solve. However, if you can just get them talking for a few seconds about their business it will give you at least a few clues as to how you can help.

- **Contact details:** If a visitor won't give you their contact details it's unlikely they're a serious prospect. If they're interested in your product and believe there's a need for it in their organisation, why would they have an issue with you getting in touch? If they say they'll take your details and get in touch with you, they probably won't.

- **Competitors:** Beware those visitors who tell you they're working with your competitor but might be looking to change. They might. But often, they're just looking for a competitive quote from you they can beat up their current supplier with. We're generally creatures of habit and getting people to move from a competitor is tough – your time may be better spent working out what you do differently to your competitors that adds more value or solves additional problems. Don't make it just about price or you're in a race to the bottom and there lies the pit of doom for both you and your competitors in the long run. Value your product and attest to the fact that it is worth the money – buy cheap buy twice!

- **Flicking through your brochure:** It might look as though they're interested but if it's just a quick flick they're not looking for more evidence as to how your product meets their needs, they're just being polite, and it will probably end up in the next bin. Likewise if they don't want to see a demo or touch/taste your product they're probably not that interested.

- **Flittering eyes:** If they're looking around, behind and away from you they're not really listening and looking out for someone or something else they can use as an excuse to get away as quickly as possible. Also, picking at a piece of fluff on their clothing or searching in their bag for something suggests their attention is elsewhere (people can be so rude!).

## Quantifying visitors

Before we look at how to identify some of the characters who might pass by your stand it's useful to think about how your squad will move through from their opening line to quantifying whether a visitor is useful to your business or not. We've discussed the ice-breaker your squad will use, whether that's an opening question, an introduction to a demonstration or an offer of a sample but where do they go after that. The following process is a helpful structure to establish whether there is the potential for future business:

- **Ice-breaker/opening question:** As per the lines you have already identified and planned to use above that will grab their initial attention.

- **Establish mutuality:** 'So what is your business involved in?' will inform you whether there are any grounds for working together. For example, if you're a seller of specialist dairy milking equipment and the visitor only farms sheep, it is unlikely you can do business together. There isn't a specific 'character' for these individuals below as they should be relatively easy to dispatch based on the fact you both realise there's little reason for pursing a conversation.

- **Establish need:** 'And is there something specific you're looking to help your business with today?' will inform you of exactly what their problem is, if they have one. For example, a dairy farmer may reply he's just setting up a second milking site and is looking for equipment to complete the fit-out.

- **Establish supply:** 'Will you be using your previous supplier to fit-out your barn?' – this opens the opportunity for the visitor to tell you what has and hasn't worked with his current supplier. This is the key listening stage to understand whether there is an issue, and if there is how your product solves it. If the dairy farmer tells you he's happy with his previous supplier and not looking to change, it's worth asking what he's particularly satisfied with – this gives you good insight into what your competitors are doing well. If you know you can offer something different to his current supplier, that adds value, it's worth introducing it now, in the context of how it could solve a problem he might not even realise he has. If however, he tells you about why he's not happy with his current provider, that's a clear signal to show him how you might be able to help.

- **Establish expectations:** 'When would you be looking to build/what budget were you thinking of investing?' – by asking questions about the purchasing process, you will be able to determine how serious the visitor is about making a future purchase. It also helps you to understand how quickly you need to move with next steps and whether the visitor is a prospect or a lead. This should also give you some clues about the buying authority of the visitor and whether there will be other people you'll need to influence before a transaction.

- **Establish next steps:** 'How would you like to move this forward?' – asking the visitor how they want to be contacted again gives you an indication of how serious a lead they are. If they respond by saying 'just send me some details over' without mentioning price, timescales, etc., it's unlikely they're in a rush to buy. However, if they're keen to pencil in a meeting and ask you to begin a detailed proposal including costs and delivery details they are much more likely to buy.

It can be easy to identify how useful a visitor is to your business based on some basic characteristics that are often on show. As with the characters in your squad, our illustrations below are extremes to make a point and often the behaviours are more subtle, but they should still give you an idea of how to spot those high-potential leads versus time-wasters.

## PASSERS-BY:

**Opera Singer**     **Tyre Kickers**     **Newbie**

**POTENTIAL FOR BUSINESS:** *LOW*     **POTENTIAL FOR ADVOCACY:** *LOW*

These are the least valuable visitors for you. They are unlikely to ever generate any sales and could cost you time and money through adding them to a newsletter distribution or CRM database where they are likely to offer you little value.

## CONTACTS:

**Competitor**     **The Expert**     **Press and Media**     **Newbie**     **Supplier**

**POTENTIAL FOR BUSINESS:** *LOW*     **POTENTIAL FOR ADVOCACY:** *LOW/MEDIUM*

Contacts may add some value to your business in saving cost, improving your offer or telling your story. However, they are unlikely to generate any sales or revenue.

## PROSPECTS:

**Interested Browsers**                    **Newbie**

**POTENTIAL FOR BUSINESS:** *MEDIUM*   **POTENTIAL FOR ADVOCACY:** *MEDIUM*

Prospects are valuable assets in adding to your sales pipeline and generating cash revenues in the future. However, as you are still building a relationship with them, they are unlikely to be strong advocates yet but by building a relationship based on their needs could become important influencers for the future.

## LEADS:

**Definite Buyers**     **Interested Browsers**     **Existing Customers**

**POTENTIAL FOR BUSINESS:** *HIGH*          **POTENTIAL FOR ADVOCACY:** *HIGH*

Leads are by far your most valuable visitors although some are more precious than others. Definite Buyers and Interested Browsers can add revenue to your business and increasingly act as advocates. Existing Customers are THE most valuable asset on the chart but are so often forgotten by exhibitors. They can significantly add to your revenue and are your biggest influencers of new customers by telling their story of how great you are to work with.

Approaching visitors can be nerve-wracking and you won't know without speaking to them exactly who a visitor is and how useful they are to you so you're going to have to break the ice – hence your amazing opening lines that we've discussed previously. Some shows colour-code badges, for exhibitors, visitors, press, speakers, etc., so as part of your preparation make sure you know if there is any differentiation between categories. Badges are also a great source of information on who someone is and their organisation, and may give clues as to what their buying authority is. However, if the first thing you do as someone walks over is squint at their badge, failing to give eye-contact, it's a giveaway you're trying to work out whether they're important or not and can feel quite impersonal. Treat everyone who approaches with the same open, direct and professional manner and use your questioning to work out who you filter them.

**Opera singer**

You can easily identify the opera singer as he uses the word 'me' a lot! He's a typical broadcaster and has all the time in the world to tell you how amazing he is, how brilliant his business is and what a wonderful holiday he had in Spain in 1986. He won't ask any questions about your product or service as he doesn't have the slightest intention of buying from you, or any of your fellow exhibitors for that matter! If he does ask you about your product, just out of courtesy, he won't pause for breath for long enough to actually let you reply before he launches in to another lengthy spiel about his life!

**Dispatch technique:** Look at your watch, apologise for interrupting, tell him politely you have an appointment due and wish him a great show.

### Tyre-kicker

Named after those faux buyers who spend afternoons walking around car showrooms, sucking in their cheeks, shaking their heads and kicking tyres with no intention of ever buying a car – unless the salesman is selling a £5,000 car for £50. They might ask lots of questions about what your product can or can't do, but only so that they are able to determine why it won't work for them or isn't the right fit. They will however gladly pocket your giveaways and brochures, saying they'll read them later with every intention of placing them in the nearest bin. They have all the time in the world to waste with you asking pointless questions, but their first one will always usually be 'So what are you giving away today then?'

**Dispatch technique:** You'll recognise them from their heaving stash of pens, earbuds, notebooks and every other freebie so make sure you have some low-value goodies at the front of your stand that you can give them as you wish them a nice show.

**Newbie**

Newbies can usually be identified by their wide-eyed, open-mouthed expressions as they survey a smorgasbord of exhibitors, every one of whom they think can help them launch their new business enterprise. They may never have attended a trade show before, or they may not have been to one for their latest entrepreneurial idea and therefore they're keen to talk to everyone, see everything that's new and take away samples and literature from everyone who may (or may not) be able to contribute to their world domination. Newbies don't really know what they're looking for and won't remember much of what you tell them

**Dispatch technique:** If you catch a newbie on their first pass of stands they may still be too excited to really listen to what you're saying and understand if you can help them. Politely move them onto the rest of the show but suggest they come back to you later in the day when they have had time to reflect on what they really need. Newbies are useful contacts to keep in touch with as they quite often have the drive and commitment to bring ideas to life and could convert to a prospect/lead in the future.

## The media

There will usually be a plethora of media folk around at trade shows from across the spectrum of consumer and trade channels, and they're usually the contacts that everyone in your squad will look to pass onto someone else! But the media are like gold dust and should be welcomed to your stand with open arms (so long as you're prepared). For more insight on how to get the most from the media see Chapter 6, but there's really nothing to fear as long as you're clear on what you want to share with them and how it benefits their audience. They can boost awareness of your proposition way beyond just the people who attend the show, through their reviews and ongoing features so don't be shy!

**Acknowledgement technique:** Hopefully you've worked out who in your squad is going to be managing the press so as soon as they approach it's time to put your PR plan into action. Equally, you'll also probably have set up some interviews and meetings so will be expecting them. As an absolute basic have a generic press release ready for any one of your squad to hand out, along with ensuring they all have a standard response available to answer any questions. And the key thing to remember, there's no such thing as off the record – so if you don't want to see it in print or on screen, don't share it!

### The expert

Every industry has its experts, some more well-known than others, who feel that they're the ultimate authority on how things should be done and what has and hasn't worked in the past. They're fairly easy to spot as they'll be the ones who will usually start the conversation with 'You know what you guys are doing wrong don't you?' before proceeding to tell you how they would have done if differently. As frustrating as experts can sometimes be, it's usually worth listening to their feedback as you never know when they might just have a nugget that solves a problem you've been struggling with, or that gives you an insight into a new customer that you hadn't thought of.

**Acknowledgement technique:** If you're working in a technical environment and you have your own expert in the squad, it's the perfect time to introduce them to each other and let them debate their respective views. If you don't and your squad are nervous of getting tied up in knots, it's worth listening and making a note of their feedback before agreeing to pass their details onto the right person to respond to them. It can be easy to lose patience with experts, so again closing it down with the excuse of a forthcoming appointment can be a useful tactic.

### The competitor

It's the perfect environment to do a bit of sneaky spying on what your competition are doing, so don't be surprised if they do the same to you! With branded uniforms, name badges and LinkedIn, it's much easier to identify your competitor these days. Before you try to march them off your stand, it might be worth engaging in conversation with them, they're probably nervous about their illicit mission and therefore might give away a few bits of tasty insight that are useful to you and your business. The key thing is to let them do the talking and don't give away too much yourself.

**Acknowledgement technique:** Admittedly you won't want your competitor hanging around your stand for too long, eyeing up your potential contacts but equally you should be confident about why your product is different and/or better so neither should you be worried about hosting them for a brief encounter. Ask them questions about how their show is going and business in general and let them talk. When you've gleaned as much as you think you're going to from them, it's always reassuring to end the conversation with 'It's been great speaking with you, but I really must go and speak with our customers who are waiting'.

## The supplier

It's the age-old complaint from exhibitors at trade shows, those 'visitors' who turn up armed with their brochure, price list and contract to try and sell to you. Event organisers have tried hard to clamp down on it over the years and most will happily intervene if you feel a supplier is being overly intrusive. But can you really blame a business that thinks it can help you, introducing themselves and trying to establish some common ground – you may even have done it yourself as a visitor at some point in time. Suppliers in general have become more discrete over the years and are happy just to leave a card and move on. You never know, maybe they can do a better job or offer a better price than your current supplier.

**Acknowledgement technique:** As with other contacts, having a clear process for dealing with suppliers will help your squad feel more comfortable in dealing with them. If you feel your business has no prospect of ever working with them, then tell them and don't share details – it will just be wasting both of your time. However, if you think there may be some potential to work together, a collaborative supplier will understand you'll have more pressing priorities at the show and look forward to hearing from you at a time that's more appropriate. If they pressure you, or fail to take the hint to move on, they're probably not the supplier for you!

### Interested browsers

Now we're getting into those juicy visitors who are interested in your product or service for all the right reasons – because they're thinking about buying from you! These are the visitors where you really do need to sharpen up on listening skills; so often the feedback from visitors intending to buy is that exhibitors don't listen to them and just trot out a standard sales pitch. Interested browsers will usually either be aware of your product (from your fantastic pre-show marketing) or have self-selected from the content of your graphics, realising they have a problem you might be able to solve by coming across your stand. They've already made the first decision that your proposition could help them in their business, but at the moment they don't have enough information to make a buying decision. Or they may not be the sole decision-maker for the buyer of your product or service. These visitors are key for investing time in, to understand what their specific issues are and for explaining how your product might help them solve it. These visitors might be few and far between but they're worth spending time with once you've found one.

**Engagement technique:** Understanding your squad's roles and responsibilities will be crucial in ensuring you maximise converting interested browsers into real prospects. These visitors are looking for information and evidence to support their buying decision so it's worth making sure they're spending time with the squad member who can provide the right answers. Interested browsers might not make a buying decision on the day but will want to confirm a follow-up action, whether that's a meeting with other members of the team, a demonstration or further commercial detail such as pricing and delivery details. It's key not to let them off the stand without knowing exactly what they're expecting next and when in terms of your relationship. Interested browsers want to know you've listened to and understand their issues so in closing off the conversation it can help to summarise it and confirm the actions. For example, 'From our conversation, I understand you're really frustrated that your IT service's standard response time is 48 hours, which is slowing down your own response time to customers. I'm going to send you our brochure which shows the options on 1-hour, 12-hour and 24-hour response times and then I'll call you next Wednesday when we can talk them through in more detail.'

Interested browsers are both today's prospects and tomorrows leads!

**Definite buyers**

The panacea of trade show visitors, the definite buyer approaches your stand with confidence, credit card or pen in hand, ready to buy or sign that big contract! They are the ones with the authority to buy. Only, it quite often doesn't quite work like that and it will all depend on whether you're actually 'selling' anything at the show itself or not. However, there will be some visitors who have done their research, have come to the show specifically looking for what you're selling and already know that you're the supplier that offers them the most effective solution. You might have a few more factors to iron out but essentially you both know from early on in the conversation that there is business to be done. The definite buyer might open a conversation by talking about volume discounts, delivery dates or minimum quantities – all very positive buying signals. They may not ask too many details about the product itself as they will likely have already done their homework and found out what they need to know.

**Engagement technique:** As with interested browsers, it's crucial to make sure that when the definite buyer leaves the stand you both know exactly what is going to happen next in the transaction. If the buyer has bought and is happily leaving with their purchase, how are you going to follow up with them to ensure they keep buying in future? If they have agreed to a sale or a proposal, how is that going to be presented and when? What do they need to see in the proposal to convert it to the final sale? Again knowing which member of your squad is most appropriate to closing out the conversation will be vital in ensuring that the lead is converted to cash.

### Existing customers

These are the ones that exhibitors quite often forget about in the quest for finding juicy new prospects. However, remember that statistic that only 16–20% of visitors are in a position to buy from you? Well, 100% of your existing customers are in a position to buy from you, so you're unlikely to meet a more receptive audience. It's much more likely, and much less expensive to expand your footprint with an existing customer than it is to recruit a new one, so ensure that you're fully maximising your existing customers throughout your pre-show, during and post-show campaigns.

**Engagement technique:** Busy stands attract visitors as we're generally quite a nosy bunch so scheduling appointments with existing clients, especially during those quieter times, can help to create a buzz. Existing customers are also great influencers in telling your story for you through social media and other channels to inspire like-minded visitors to pay your stand a visit. However, remember how you felt when you saw your bank or mobile operator offering a sexy deal for new customers but gave you nothing for your loyalty? Avoid making your customers feel the same by ensuring you have a range of offers and services for both new and existing customers – although you've already done business they'll still appreciate you adding value. And if nothing else, talking to strangers all day can be exhausting, so the sight of a friendly face can be hugely invigorating.

There are probably countless other examples of visitors we could also include, from students to investors to futurologists, but hopefully these characters give you some useful reference points to help identify where you should be spending most of your precious time on the stand. The two key things with any visitor are to manage expectations and confirm next steps. Visitors and exhibitors are busy people and there is nothing more frustrating for both parties than pursuing a relationship that clearly doesn't have any mutual benefit – it is just time-wasting for both parties. Being clear about whether there is an opportunity, and explicit about what that opportunity is, enables both parties to embark on building a relationship that results in a problem being solved. Equally frustrating is having held a good conversation but not knowing where it goes next, or worse still never hearing from each other again – agreeing what comes next ensures that there are no surprises and creates a positive impression for the future. And as we'll discuss in the next chapter, if you've made a commitment to follow-up, just do it!

*Eighty-one per cent of trade show visitors have buying authority – Which means more than 4 out of 5 prospects and leads are decision makers about buying your product-Source: Exhibitors Survey Inc.*
(XL Displays, 2017)

## Summary

Although we've called this section of P.I.E. Implementation because it's all about what happens on-site, you'll see that a huge slice of it needs to happen in your planning time before getting delivered on-site. All the time you spent planning the perfect stand and inviting the ideal prospects goes to waste if your stand squad don't know what they're doing to identify visitors when they arrive.

So as you think about how your stand and squad will perform on the day, here are some summary questions that will help sharpen up your thinking and ensure you bring the best out of every resource you've got.

- How much time do you personally need on-site during build-up to ensure that everything is operating as it should and that you're show-ready?

- How many squad members do you need for the size of your stand?

- Which different characters can you identify in the squad you have available? What weakness and strength does this give you and how can you mitigate or maximise it via additional training?

- How will your squad first engage with visitors – what's your opening line?

- How, where and when will you train your squad? What are the key areas you need to include?

- Who is your ideal customer? How will your squad identify them?

- What's the process for filtering visitors to ensure that you identify the ones who can help you achieve your objectives?

- How comfortable are your team in dispatching passers-by and contacts and how can you help them?

Now you've done all the hard work and it's just the follow-up to go – the easy bit! Amazingly 87% of exhibitors never follow-up with visitors they met at trade shows (Schroeder, 2012) – and then wonder why they don't get any business as a result. Actually, up to now has been the easy bit and this is where the hard work really starts. Following up and evaluating the success of your show are the key components that will determine whether you invest in any future events and they're a crucial part of the mix!

# CHAPTER 5

# EVALUATION

*You won't get different results as long as you continue doing what you do, and in the manner which you are doing it. Change something!*
—Akiroq Brost, writer

Congratulations, you've made it! You might have aching feet, tired calves and a rasping throat but you've made it to the end of show, you're still alive and all your hard work has paid off – or has it? Just because the show has closed to visitors doesn't mean your job is done unfortunately, in fact this is where the hard work really starts, converting all those prospects and leads into profits. In addition to executing a finely tuned follow-up campaign, now's the time to really understand what did and didn't work for you and what you can do better next time – if a next time is even the right thing for your business to be investing in.

## 5.1 Breakdown

It's so easy to run for the door when the claxon goes to signal the end of a show, but who's going to make sure your kit and equipment gets home safely and all those hard-fought-for leads end up back in the office? The breakdown phase isn't usually given much thought in the planning process but there are some key elements that are worth considering once the show floor is clear of visitors.

## Closing time

In the many exhibitions we've been at over the years, we've often had a wager running between the stand squad on what the earliest pack-up time will be, and which exhibitors will crack first. You can usually notice it from about lunchtime on the last day, with a noticeable increase in avid clock-watching as the hands creep around to closing time. The earliest we've seen an exhibitor breakdown (the stand, not themselves) was 2.30pm for a show that closed at 5.00pm. Inevitably this has a domino effect as every other exhibitor presumes it's now acceptable to pack away their stand and within about half an hour there was a sea of empty shells down one aisle. Even worse, the shell scheme crew took this as their signal to start dismantling the structures at 4.00pm so with an hour to go, not only did you have empty shells, there were empty aisles. The unfortunate thing for the first in this domino effect was that at 4.30pm a party of four buyers came into the show who had been unexpectedly held up and had come with the sole intention of seeing the exhibitor in question. To say that they were incensed with the whole situation is an understatement and any existing goodwill between the two parties evaporated – who knows what deals the exhibitor ultimately lost out on?

On the final day, the squad will be tired and the aisles will be quieter, but who's to say that the hottest prospect you're going to meet isn't going to walk into the show half an hour before close, as was the case above? It never reflects well on your brand and can show a lack of respect for organisers and visitors if you're more interested in getting things put away in cardboard boxes than talking to visitors. That's not to say you can't put that quieter time to good use by talking to your squad about their feedback and ideas, letting any spare team members have a walk around to see other exhibitors or having a general tidy up of your area. Just don't start stripping walls, unplugging screens and swapping unused stock with other exhibitors, it just looks unprofessional! Trade visitors especially do not appreciate seeing suppliers swapping stock. Many retailers have commented to us in the past that it's disrespectful to them as customers because the very same suppliers have pleaded poverty when it comes to margins on their products, yet they allow staff to give away product for their own gain at these events.

You might be tempted to book the first train/plane home after the show closes, but realistically you'll have a bit of work to do packing up, even if your stand-builders are doing the majority of it, so why not give yourself a bit of extra time and if you get chance for a relaxed drink before heading home, even better!

## Security

During both build-up and breakdown there are lots of people walking around from lots of different businesses and it's a prime time for things to go missing. We'd like to say that it's just a case of contractors borrowing each other's kit to get the job done, and often it can be. However, there can often be less scrupulous individuals about and if they have a high-vis jacket and a lanyard on, they're probably not going to get challenged too harshly about why they're wheeling a 58-inch TV screen out to a van. Although you may have packed everything up into neat boxes and left it on your stand for your courier to collect, if you're not there to hand it over there's no guarantee that someone else won't walk off with it. It's not just kit and equipment we've seen go missing, laptops can be left unattended allowing a competitor to slip a USB stick in and access a price list or other commercially sensitive information. Breakdown is a prime time for things going missing, so if you want to be absolutely sure your kit, equipment and information ends up where it should do, stick with it until it's collected and don't leave anything to chance.

This is again another reason for smaller exhibitors to ensure that they have two people on the event. One of you can stay with your gear while the other patiently waits in line with your vehicle for a slot in one of the loading bays and you then both can take turns ferrying your stand's contents once you have your parking space. A point to remember at this stage is that due to the limited space around loading bays, many venues have a deposit system whereby you hand over cash to enable access to this area for a nominal hour. If you don't redeem your voucher within the hour you may have just lost upwards of £50 for a car or small van. The charges for lorries and large vans is much more but you get proportionally more time for the privilege.

## Recycling

As we mentioned in the section on stand design, the more you can produce that can be reused at future events the better – not only does it create consistency for visitors it also cuts down on costs. However, we have seen situations where squad members, thinking they're being helpful, have ripped down graphics panels in a rush to get out, only to discover the plan was to use them at subsequent shows. If you are thinking of using any of your stand collateral in future, make sure everyone knows what's getting binned and what's for keeping. The logistics of getting your kit back to your base will no doubt have been thought through as part of the planning process, but having a clear exit plan for exactly what's going where and with whom will help you all get away speedily.

If you're a food and drink producer, samples can often be an issue, especially if you've been generous with your ordering. Often organisers will have a nominated charity to donate any spare samples to, while venue staff and other exhibitors can usually be relied on to get rid of excess stocks. We have seen occasions where suppliers have been desperately ringing their logistics teams on the final day trying to get someone to come and pick up all the spare samples they haven't used, and it can become costly. Venues will often have a new exhibition moving into your space as soon as you ship out, so they simply don't have the capacity to be storing excess stock from exhibitors. Anything that gets left on a stand or in a storage area after the designated time will be disposed of, so if you think you're going to need to get rid of some spare stock at the end of the show, the sooner you can work on a plan the better.

## Logistics

Often in the excitement of planning how to get your kit to the venue for the show, getting it home again can be forgotten and where you might presume you've agreed this as part of your stand-build process, you could be mistaken! A full box of brochures can get delivered along with the stand, but has anyone thought about who's taking the leftovers home – are they going back into storage until the next show or back to the office where the sales team might be able to make use of them? We'll discuss considerations for international events in the next section, but have you considered if your stand will get back to base in time for the next show you need it at or is it better to send it directly onto the next country and store it there? The logistics of getting your kit out and back to wherever you're keeping it, factoring in storage costs, are just as important as getting it there.

## Leads

How upset would you be if you got back into the office ready to follow up all those juicy, promising leads only to find that they've been left behind at the show and subsequently thrown out by the venue? Don't think that never happens – it does, and more frequently than you might think! If its hard copy leads you've collected, make sure someone is responsible for them, and that they know they are. If you're collecting leads electronically, check you know how to access them and that they're stored safely until the time you can actually do something with them. Bottom line, just don't forget them!

### 5.2 Follow-up

Ask yourself just for a moment what this has all been about. The months of planning, of making tough decisions, of selecting the best people, of training them and then spending days with painful feet and tired eyes, engaging with a bunch of random strangers. Hopefully it was all about connecting with the right people who you have the potential to build a relationship with that leads to profitable sales growth for your company. If you're reading that and thinking it's some other reason, then maybe you've been at the wrong event! But if it is about growing sales, that's not going to happen just because you met someone – there's a whole series of things that need to happen before cash actually changes hands and most of them need to be driven by you. And if cash doesn't ever change hands, how can you expect to get any meaningful payback on your investment?

*Only 13% of leads from trade shows are ever followed up, yet over half of all visitors make a purchase within 12 months of visiting a show.*
(Davis, 2014)

Are you surprised that 87% of leads are never followed up? I'll say that again, only 13% of exhibitors ever follow up with the contacts that they made at a trade show. Yet over half of all visitors make a purchase from an exhibitor they met within 12 months of a show. Just imagine how much more business could be done if only exhibitors followed up on all those leads they collected. Just by following up and keeping in contact with people, you're already being more effective than 87% of your fellow exhibitors. Relationships are built on trust, so failing to deliver on a promise you made at a trade show already impacts negatively on the relationship you're trying to build and reflects badly on your brand.

## Who captures leads?

As we mentioned in the squad section of the previous chapter, who is responsible for collecting your data and leads will depend on your circumstances and resources, but whatever you decide to do, make sure your team know what they're responsible for. If you're employing a squad member as a stand host to greet visitors and do some initial filtering, it is essentially their role to collect the details of those visitors who may be useful contacts (e.g., media, suppliers) before passing on prospects and leads to other members of the team. As we've mentioned, avoid the pressure of feeling you have to collect details of passers-by if there is genuinely no potential for any type of business relationship. If you're employing this method, it can be tempting for a stand host to scan absolutely everyone that passes to get as many contacts as they can (possibly justifying their role) but this kind of drive-by scanning can result in a host of random, unqualified leads that serve as a distraction when it comes to following up.

Where you only have a couple of squad members on the stand you're likely to be equally involved in recording details regardless of whether the visitor is a contact, prospect or lead. Again, part of the squad training process is ensuring that you are both confident that you know what you're recording, how you're recording it and where you're storing those leads to follow up on. If you have a larger squad and will be handing over prospects and leads to your sales or other colleagues, it becomes their responsibility to collect the relevant details to keep in touch. This isn't without its challenges, especially if those squad members are from your sales team. Salespeople are successful because of their motivation, and personal drive, so if they've netted a red-hot lead at a show it might be difficult getting them to share it with the rest of the team. As a salesperson it's absolutely right that they should follow up and convert the business- as long as they do. It's equally important, however, they let you know the value of the business they've converted so that you can build that into evaluating the ROI. In addition, on a personal level, the more responsibility you can take for bringing new business to your company, the more likely your peers will see you as part of the strategic sales process as opposed to 'just an event organiser'. The amount of new business that has been unlocked due to the strategic planning, thought and attention to detail you have put into trade show campaigns is vast and if you have promotion aspirations, trade shows create valuable evidence for you to talk about in an interview.

Whoever is going to have responsibility for capturing details on your stand, include it as part of your training so your squad know what they're responsible for and how they will action what you're asking them to do. If you can remember all the way back to the start of the process where we discussed setting objectives, we talked about how quality was more important than quantity, which is key to emphasise to your team. It only takes three or four visitors that can deliver quality business for your organisation to get your show investment back. Leaving the show with thousands, even hundreds of contact names isn't success if you don't know who they are, what their needs are and whether your products and services form part of the solution. The culture of trade shows historically has been to judge success on how many new names you've collected, but this can be a lazy way of measuring the wrong metric. You might be surprised how empowered your team feel if you give them the freedom not to chase phone numbers.

If you execute your trade show lead strategy correctly, you can ensure:

- You never miss a hot lead because your squad are fully trained and prepared.

- You don't let warm leads slip away.

- Everyone who has contact with your squad knows who you are and how you can help.

- You maximise your ROI for the remainder of the year.

## Post-show lead management

Just as important as capturing those leads will be planning for the post-show management and tracking of them. It may well be that the hot prospects and leads will fall to you, but you also need to keep a track on what has happened to the rest. In many instances, once leads have been handed over to the sales team, they seem to fall into a black hole, leaving exhibit managers unable to track those leads and, as a result, unable to prove that their hard work has actually delivered any bottom-line benefits. If you can flag these elusive prospects and leads through an established CRM system that can then keep you in the loop, all well and good, but if not, you will need to come up with a workable reporting procedure that can inform and update their progression.

*Only 47% of companies track leads generated at trade shows and events throughout the sales cycle, and only 28% measure and report the number of leads that ultimately convert to sales as part of their exhibit programs' ROI.*
*(Exhibitor Media Group research sponsored by Lynch Exhibits Inc. and In4med Corp)*

## Follow-up process

Once you've got all these leads and you're back in the office what do you do next? As we've said before, as long as you just do something, you'll be ahead of 87% of other exhibitors at the show. The first day back in the office after a trade show can be a welcome relief from all the stand plans, squad training and logistics planning that will inevitably have eaten up your time in the weeks prior to the show. Equally, having had a few days on-site, with emails and calls stacking up, you'll probably be eager to do anything but think about the show it's so tempting to retreat back to the day-job, thinking you'll put your follow-up plan into action tomorrow. However, so often we've heard stories where tomorrow has drifted into the day after, then the week after and then never actually happens. It's so easy to just forget about it once you're onto the next project. If you can, book an afternoon into your diary as soon after the show as possible to start your follow-up and be disciplined enough to stick to it. Some exhibitors stay an extra night close to the venue and use the peace and quiet of a hotel room the following morning to tackle their plan. Working on the basis that what gets measured gets done, consider adding follow-up as one of your SMART objectives – it's something you're in control of and able to measure.

Whichever method of data capture you've chosen from the options detailed in Chapter 3, hopefully you'll have built in some categorisation so that you're not just faced with a random collection of contact details when you do sit down to follow-up. If you haven't, well you've just learnt a valuable lesson for next time. Gone are the days when everyone you met gets the standard company response, increasingly we're expecting tailored, personalised communications that show we've been listened to and that add value. That doesn't mean that every single person has an individual response (although you probably do want to do that for prospects and leads) but certainly within categories the message, frequency and call to action will be different depending on where they are in the buying journey.

So how do you deal with the different categories of visitors that you've met?

- **Passers-by:** The first question would be why have you even collected their details? If there is absolutely no prospect of you ever working together in any capacity is it really worth keeping in touch? You might think it's useful to add them to your company database for the automated newsletter. Sure, it's not much resource for you, it boosts your circulation details and well, you just never know! There is a small shred of logic in that, but equally if the newsletter is just going into their spam folder, or isn't getting read, or isn't prompting the action you're suggesting, then it's just diluting the effectiveness of your hard work. You want high open-rates of your newsletter, good click-throughs to your website and calls to your telesales team – sending out communications to hundreds of people who are never going to do these things just weakens the results of your ongoing marketing campaigns. Don't be afraid to bin contact details of passers-by who add no value to your business. You're not at trade shows to make friends, you're paying for the opportunity to find fans who will contribute to the growth of your business.

- **Contacts:** You'll probably find that the majority of details you collect fall into this category, people who might be useful in the future, either as a potential buyer, a collaborator or a supplier. There definitely needs to be some follow-up with them but it can be a more generic communication, although not as generic as sending the same group email out to everyone. For example, with the media you might want to send individual journalists an email introducing them to the relevant PR person in your team whose responsibility it is to follow up with them. For suppliers, again you might send an email sharing details of your organisation's procurement policy or asking them to forward samples of their work. Newbies are a group where, depending on the conversation, you may want to tailor your conversation based on their circumstances and encourage them to keep in touch with updates on how their business is progressing.

- **Prospects:** Depending on the resource you have available it may be you that's following up with prospects, or potentially they will have been handed over to your sales team. If you're in control of the contact it's simply a case of ensuring that whatever was agreed as the next steps (e.g., sending pricing, samples, agreeing a next meeting) actually happens and you help them move along the buying journey towards becoming a lead. If you've handed over the details to a sales colleague, it's worth following up yourself also to acknowledge and thank them for their time at the show and let them know what will happen next. This broadens your company's exposure to them and gives them more than one touchpoint. It also means they have someone else to follow-up with should the sales team fail to initiate contact. As you evaluate the show over the next couple of months it also gives you an opportunity to engage with them and get their feedback on your execution and what more they would have wanted to see from your stand.

- **Leads:** The ones that everyone wants to follow-up, the perceived low-hanging fruit that are quick and easy to convert. These visitors always deserve an individual, tailored response focusing exactly on the discussion you've had about how your product or service meets their needs and how the transaction will progress from here. Again, there's no harm in sending an acknowledgement email with the details of who is going to follow-up with them if it isn't yourself, and an outline of the next steps. It may take some time to gather all the information a prospect or lead has requested but don't wait until you have everything ready to make contact with them – they could think you've forgotten them and bought from your competitor while they were waiting. Let them know you're working on their requests and give them a timescale of when you'll be able to provide the missing information they've asked for – and stick to it! The follow-up from visitors to exhibitors is as equally low, so visitors are unlikely to initiate contact with a supplier despite how keen they seemed in conversation at the show, so never rely on them to get in touch – they probably won't without a prompt.

Having reviewed the contact details you've collected you should have a clear idea of who is getting which response and from whom and you're all ready to start making contact – but what do you say? Before we get into some of the ideas for keeping in touch, the first thing to remember is to keep saying it. One of the key criticisms of trade shows is that nothing comes from the contacts that have been made, but so often that's after one email or direct mail fails to get a response. While a visitor may have seemed enthusiastic and excited about your proposition while you were talking, they've also gone back to their day job after the show and a ton of other priorities to deal with. They will have received hundreds of emails in between speaking to you and receiving yours and you're just not top of their mind anymore. So, don't be disheartened if you don't get anything back first time around, and don't give up. Just keep reminding them about how you solve their problem, keep being useful by adding value and build trust in your expertise. It's going to take time and effort, but for the right prospects and leads it will ultimately be worth it. Once you realise the effort that goes into converting a warm lead it might be easier to understand why you just don't have the time or resource to waste on hundreds of cold ones.

Research has shown that it will take on average seven touchpoints with an organisation before a buyer is fully committed to moving towards a purchase decision. A touchpoint could be something as simple as a retweet or a joining a conversation on social media, it might be sharing a link to a blog that you think could be useful or it might be sending a white paper on a topic you've discussed. Research also suggests that even for your hottest leads, around 40% won't be in a position to buy right now, and there will be a period of consolidation and discussion before any business is done. Therefore, the whole aim of ongoing contact is to build the relationship based on showing how you can make their life easier and more efficient. Hopefully, for prospects you've already identified as interesting, the first touchpoint will have happened before the show even opened with either a VIP invitation or a social media approach so you're already onto touchpoint three or four by the time you're working on following up.

Here's an example of how a seven-touch follow-up process can work for prospect and lead conversion:

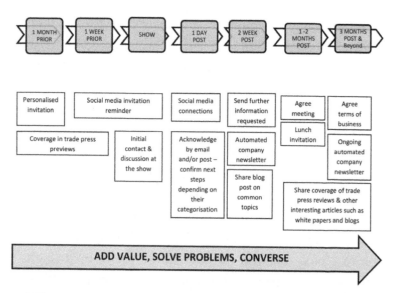

Wherever you can, think about the content for your post-show follow-up campaign as part of your planning process, creating an aligned, value-adding and consistent campaign that is relevant for visitors. There's nothing worse than sitting down knowing you have prospects and leads to talk to and staring at a blank page. Equally, it can give you a reason to talk to visitors about how you're going to follow up if you're not sure where to take the conversation. For example, write a white paper or create new instruction videos of how to use your equipment, and have those ready to share after the show as a reason to keep in touch – you can show how you'll add value to them going forward as opposed to just chasing a sale. If you want to test how hot a lead is, ask them to complete a specific action such as 'downloading a white paper' rather than just sending it in an email – for those visitors who are really engaged with what you have to say, a few clicks won't be an issue and you can be confident they want to know more from you.

Here are some other areas you might want to consider for your follow-up process:

- **Refresh their memory:** Visitors will have met hundreds of exhibitors, and while you may have had a positive conversation, they're unlikely to remember you. Use a photograph of your stand while it was busy and include that in the email/newsletter to remind them of who you are.

- **Give them exposure:** Write a blog reviewing your experience at the show and include comments about how much you enjoyed meeting them, or what you learned from them. Include their social media tags when sharing the blog post to boost their exposure and create some awareness for them.

- **Surprise them:** Was there a common interest or something unusual that you discussed that you could use as a reason to show you were really listening? For example, we once had a discussion with a prospect who was a fellow AC/DC fan who hadn't read the singer's autobiography based around his love of cars, which we'd just really enjoyed. So we sent him a copy with a note saying, 'Hope this gives you some light relief amongst the day job' – he became a client and subsequent conversations were often started with 'Do you remember that bit where…?'. If you have some high value prospects and leads that are worth investing in, why not follow up with a high-value offer or product that they weren't expecting. For example, if you think there is scale and lifetime value with a contact, can you offer a free upgrade to a more premium version, or complimentary training or service packages? Something that is relevant and of high perceived value that keeps them invested in your business will help to build the relationship.

- **Get to the point:** Although research would suggest visitors aren't going to be inundated with follow-up emails from exhibitors, they will be busy after taking time out for the show. So keep the initial contact short and to the point – remind them who you are, what you agreed and what's going to happen next. Don't always presume you know what they need – closing out the acknowledgement email with 'How can I help you further?' or 'What more information can we provide to help you reach a decision?' ensures that they're not inundated with what you think is useful and focuses on moving them along the buying journey. Try to put the ball back into the visitor's court by motivating them to act, rather than just sending an email that tells them again how brilliant you think your product is.

- **Non-visitors:** Did you contact people in your pre-marketing that you didn't actually meet? This is an opportunity to follow up with them and find out whether they even attended the show and if not, what were their reasons – this give you some insight about whether you were at the right show. Equally, if they did attend but didn't come and see you, why was that? Can you share some of the content from the show, so they understand what they missed and how you can help?

- **Newsletter content:** In your planning, work out what coverage from the show you will need for the first newsletter that's going out after the show. That might be video testimonials from visitors who have had a great experience at your stand, images of a busy stand, highlights from a keynote speaker or details of the high-profile visitors or journalists you met. Don't leave to chance that someone might get some interesting footage that you can use – decide what you need and make sure you capture it.

- **Influencing others:** If you're wanting visitors to influence other buyers, for example journalists through the trade press or bloggers directly to your audience, how will you communicate with them to make sure they follow up on any promises they gave you about coverage while at the show? They will have seen lots of other exhibitors, visitors and industry stakeholders during the event so potentially could have forgotten all about you, so think of a creative way to remind them how much their audience want to hear about you!

- **Get creative:** Emails are the obvious, efficient and low-cost way of following up with contacts, but they aren't always the most effective. If you can remember as far back as Chapter 1, you'll have learned that over 269 billion emails are sent every day, of which half never even reach their recipient. So even if your email does reach the right person, are you going to catch them at the right moment for them to absorb what you're saying, or think about the next steps, among a sea of other emails? Getting back to basics, trade shows are all about face-to-face interaction and an opportunity to speak to people, so pick up the phone, arrange a coffee, send them a video message – for the leads you really want to convert, think about ways to communicate that will disrupt, engage and amuse your target enough to make them want to keep building a relationship with you. Your less knowledgeable fellow exhibitors are likely to simply send a generic email to every contact on their list, so you need to think about how yours will disrupt and engage to cut through any other noise.

- **Subject lines:** If you are sending an email, think about what you put in the subject line. So much time, effort and thought goes into the content of the body of an email without any real attention to what goes in the subject line, often with the default 'Follow-up to trade show', which lacks any real standout. Getting personal and using the recipient's name in the subject line is a great start, along with adding a question such as 'John, did you make it home safely from the IMETYOU Show last week?'. Using something totally unrelated to your product or service but asking a more general question is likely to make more impact in grabbing someone's attention. If you're looking for something formal for your industry you could try 'Alex, did you find the solution to your widget problem at IMETYOU last week?' – again showing empathy and understanding of the reasons they were at the show. If questions aren't for you, try using a 'Highlights' approach, e.g., 'Five things we learnt from IMETYOU last week', which should engage with a reader to check they haven't missed anything (we all hate missing out). And if all else fails, rhymes, alliteration and puns can help but watch you don't veer into the realms of cliché or irrelevance.

While your priority focus will be on following up with leads and the hottest of prospects it's easy to forget about those contacts and cooler prospects that you're also wanting to move along the buying process. You might not have the resource to create individual, tailored contact plans for each of them but a general communication strategy including frequent newsletters, product announcements and trade press coverage will help keep you on their radar. Using social media to be part of an ongoing conversation with them, or inviting them to forthcoming trade shows or events you're attending are all reasons to keep reminding them of who you are and how you might be able to help – but make the comms plan as generic and light on resource as possible until you've received some stronger signals they they're in a position to start considering making a purchase.

 *How long after the show do exhibitors convert sales from prospects leads?*

| | |
|---|---|
| *Less than 3 months* | 14% |
| *3 to 6 months* | 17% |
| *7 to 11 months* | 19% |
| *12 to 18 months* | 29% |
| *19 months to 2 years* | 10% |
| *Over 2 years* | 2% |
| *Don't know* | 9% |

> 50% sales return within 11 months on trade show leads

*(Michael Hughes, vice-president, research and consulting, Tradeshow Week Magazine)*

Remember following the show your goal is to generate business from your top leads. Maximising your results simply requires the implementation of a systematic seven touch-point process and smart use of your time and resources executed over the post three-month show period. This will gain you some initial sales, but it will also build a platform from which to continue the dialogue with your leads because, as shown above, most buyers say that they don't actually purchase from an exhibitor until at least three months after the initial contact. So, don't get disheartened if you don't generate quick results, nurture those leads and benefit from listening and creating a personal connection.

 *Twelve per cent of exhibitors continue ongoing comms with nonresponsive leads indefinitely as part of a 'lead nurturing' strategy to maintain top-of-mind awareness with those prospects.*
(*Exhibitor Media Group research sponsored by Lynch Exhibits Inc. and In4med Corp*)

*To build a long-term successful enterprise, when you don't close a sale, open a relationship.*
—Patricia Fripp, author, executive speech coach, keynote speaker, sales presentation skills trainer, online learning expert

## So not quite as easy as just dropping out a few emails and crossing your fingers then?

More often than not, the burning question that senior management are seeking and hounding you for as soon as the show closes is what was the return on investment (ROI)? Following up professionally and effectively takes time, resource and commitment (like anything with trade shows) but it's the single most important thing you'll do in relation to the whole event and it's the crucial element that will give you the basis to your answers regarding ROI, which will be addressed further on in this chapter.

If you don't follow up, what was the point of any of the rest of it? The more you can plan before the show, the easier and less overwhelming it will seem when you're tired at the end of the show while also ensuring you've got everything in place to execute your plan like a pro. And remember, just by doing something you'll already be ahead of the 87% of your fellow exhibitors who opted out of this phase!

## 5.3 Evaluation

So, if no one (or not many) visitors are actually spending money with you at the show itself, how – and more importantly when – do you start to evaluate how successful it's been? It's a great question and one where trade shows come in for easy criticism from senior management teams who want to know exactly how much business has been generated as soon as possible. Accurate evaluation takes time and if relationships are built to generate sales for several years, it might be impossible to ever truly measure the scale of the return. Since trade shows are so difficult to evaluate, it provides excuse enough for many exhibitors just to shake their head, say it's not possible and go do exactly the same thing again next year and the year after with no better results. However, there are useful and legitimate ways you can evaluate the whole trade show process and find the evidence that helps you to make better informed and more effective decisions for the next event you're investing in – it just takes time and effort, like everything else when executing effective trade shows.

There are two key elements to comprehensive evaluation of trade shows that will give you a good insight in to the true ROI of your activity – feedback and measurement. Feedback will give you more qualitative insight into what worked and what didn't and how you can change things going forward, whereas measurement will appeal more to those looking for a quantitative output from the show's success. Used collectively, feedback and measurement should give you a good overall picture of how hard your investment has worked, in the context of the many variables that operate in the trade show environment.

## Feedback

Feedback is a gift, so they say, but from bitter personal experience we know how disheartening it can be when you've put so much time and effort in delivering a trade show to hear people tell you how they would have done it better. There are so many unknowns, variables and unexpected twists with trade shows that there will always be something you could do better and when you're so busy you don't always see it. The fact you've put so much thought and planning in is an achievement in itself, and some of the feedback you receive you'll be able to dismiss, knowing there were legitimate reasons why you can't do what someone is suggesting – yes flying a bird of prey above your stand could have been a great way of articulating the message that your company is 'eagle-eyed' but when you asked, the venue's 'no live animals' policy prevented you from doing that! And I'm sure some visitors will tell you that your stand would have been much more successful had you had comfy sofas, Wi-Fi and a free bar – trust us, unless that's what your business is selling, it wouldn't. Get as much feedback as you can, take on-board what you think is fair, but discount the noise that doesn't add value because it is just noise.

## Squad

Your squad are a fantastic source of insight (and the most accessible) as to what worked, what didn't and how you can improve your overall proposition for next time. Bear in mind the comments we have made previously about the subjective nature of stand design and overall trade show execution and accept that some will just be opinion, but in among that there should be some nuggets from a different perspective that are valuable.

In seeking feedback from your squad, ask them:

- **Was it the right show?** From the conversations they had with visitors, were they expecting to see your organisation at the show? What had visitors been looking to buy in general at the show and how ready were they to buy? This insight should give you a clear indication, regardless of your own personal performance, of whether the audience were the right one for you to be targeting.

- **How did the stand work logistically?** From an operational perspective, was the stand easy to work and did visitors understand what you did from the graphics? Things will inevitably emerge during the show that you hadn't anticipated that just make running the show more difficult. If you're using the same stand design again for another show it's particularly important to capture this feedback and put it right to make it easier for everyone next time around. This isn't about whether one of your squad would have preferred a blue stand to a green one, but about how easy it was to work operationally.

- **What were other exhibitors doing better/differently?** As we've mentioned, those quieter times are a great opportunity for your squad to have a look around at what everyone else is doing and pick up insight on what others are executing that's having more of an impact in engaging with visitors. If imitation is the highest form of flattery then don't be scared of taking a good idea from someone else and incorporating it into your stand; at the end of the day they would be looking to do the same if the boot was on the other foot!

- **What opportunities did you miss?** No matter how many times you've run trade shows, even the same event, there's always something that you've missed or can learn from. As you'll be so busy running the stand during the show, your squad are the perfect observers to tell you what other events, networking, marketing or display opportunities there are that you could benefit from at the next show.

- **How well did the squad training and management work?** You want to make the whole process as easy and relaxed as possible for your squad to put in their very best performance, so again, don't be scared of asking them about how things worked and how you could make the whole experience work better for them. Feedback for this element needs to be captured soon after the event but subsequently it may also be incorporated as part of their appraisal cycle and you may need to pass on a review of their performance to their line manager, if that isn't you of course.

- **What surprised you?** What did they get asked about that they weren't expecting? Great planning will have hopefully minimised the risk of too many difficult surprises either from a product or stand perspective but there are bound to have been a few. Identifying them now should help to alleviate them at future shows.

- **How effective was your sales pitch?** For conversations with prospects and leads, how well did the product pitch go? Did visitors easily understand what problem your product solved and how it fit into their business? If it didn't, what were the stumbling blocks and were there any frequent questions coming up that you didn't have the answers for? This doesn't only help shape your communications for the next show, it might highlight gaps across your entire product proposition that you had missed or weren't communicating clearly enough. On a more positive note, which selling points resonated most strongly with visitors and how can you use those within your ongoing comms to really enhance your product's value?

## Exhibitors

No doubt you'll have made friends with your neighbours and fellow exhibitors during the course of the show, so why not get in touch afterwards and ask them for their thoughts? Find out about their experience of the show overall, what the quality of visitors was like on their stand and how satisfied they are with the leads they picked up. They might also be able to give you some feedback on what they thought of your stand and ideas for things you could do differently. If you see a stand you really like, or that has been particularly busy, ask the event organisers for that exhibitor's contact details and get in touch to get their perspective on how they run successful events. Your fellow exhibitors will usually be pleased to hear from you and interested about sharing their thoughts with someone else who understands what they've just gone through.

## Visitors

The most important people at the show are the visitors and the most useful feedback as to whether your stand, message and proposition is influential is from visitors. If possible incorporate a way of capturing data on the stand from visitors as to their thoughts on how well they understand the graphic's contents, whether they were expecting you to be represented at the show and how well the squad have met their needs. This could be through simple exit interviews that you could ask one of your squad to complete as people leave, or through a tablet self-questionnaire for a reward. If you don't manage to capture feedback on-site, there's always an opportunity to send a Survey Monkey link out with the follow-up emails, although if visitors aren't that invested in your company they may not be motivated to respond (why would they?). The easiest way is to set an objective for each of your squad to select a certain number of contacts per day and ask them if they consent to a short telephone follow-up in the next week to ask them some questions about the show. Giving some space between the show and contacting visitors gives you a view on how memorable your stand is. If your business has a telesales team then this is an easy way to collect responses by giving them a short script, otherwise if you're doing it yourself it shouldn't take more than hour. You only really need 5–10 minutes from around 6–8 visitors to get enough valuable insight to help inform your evaluation. Again, quality is better than quantity so seven great conversations that give you something to work with is better than 200 quick calls that all give you the same top-line critique.

## Stand designers

If you have used a stand designer and builder, don't forget to add them to your feedback cycle. Ask them about how they thought they whole process worked, where the budget pinch points were, any areas where the build was more difficult than they expected or where the stand didn't operate as they anticipated at the show. They will have worked on hundreds of stand builds over the years and witnessed hundreds more in operation so again they will be a great source of information about what you can do to make the whole process easier, quicker and more effective in the future.

## Event organisers

You will probably be involved in an ongoing dialogue with the event organisers as they try and get you to sign up for the following year but make sure they're giving you the evidence you need to help make your decision about rebooking. Event organisers can be reluctant to give away too many details about attendance rates but in the interests of making a decision in their favour they should be able to share some metrics with you about how many people registered, how many actually attended, average time spent at the show, etc. Also ask them about what they thought the strengths and weaknesses of the show were and how they're thinking they may address them in future. It's always interesting to see if they have picked up on the same things as you did about what didn't work and how open they are to hear your ideas about how you can change them. A good event organiser will be eager to have this dialogue with you as they will be using it within their own follow-up process.

How you collect feedback from these different sources will depend on the resource you have available and how broad and deep you want to go in understanding the whole trade show execution. However, it's advisable to try and complete the feedback-gathering stage as soon after the show as possible, as everyone will move back to the day job and soon forget about what they saw, heard and took away from the show.

## Measurement

Where you do have a little more time is in measuring the outputs and outcomes of the trade show, especially as some of the metrics will take time to emerge. There are undoubtedly some things you can measure from the day after the show closes, but as we've talked about in this chapter, converting leads to sales can take time, 40% coming between three and 11 months after the show. If you don't know when all the leads will be converted how can you ever calculate an accurate ROI, that annoying metric that people are always so interested in knowing about trade shows?

The starting point is knowing what you're going to measure, which should come from all the time working on those SMART objectives right at the start of the process. Knowing what you were trying to achieve in the first place gives you a great head-start on working out how effective everything else was.

Establish whether you're measuring outputs or outcomes, as each will have a different metric attached to judging success.

- **Output:** What actually happened in terms of the event itself.

- **Outcome:** Behaviour that was driven as a result of the output.

For example, an output may be that you collected contact details and detailed information on seven hot leads during the show. The outcome is that four of those leads converted to customers with a collective sales value of £100,000. Or an output could be that the company was featured in the show preview of two of the leading industry magazines. An outcome would be that ten new contacts visited your stand directly as a result of reading about the business in the magazine (this one might be difficult to measure but it may be that visitors mention that they read about you, or you could use a special offer code in different magazines that customers can use to redeem on the stand to identify themselves). Outputs can usually be calculated more quickly than outcomes, which can take longer to emerge.

## What to measure

The metrics you decide to measure will depend on the resource you have available, the SMART objectives you set and how your business wants to determine success. It may even be different for different shows, but in a trade environment it's unlikely to be as simple as a cash revenue number. However, some of the metrics you could choose to measure that would be useful include:

- **Total visitor numbers to your stand:** This can be a bit of a vanity measure as the number alone doesn't give any indication of how useful those visitors are. It also ties up resource with usually one person responsible for recording the tally of visitors. However, for some companies this is an important metric that still needs recording.

- **Visitors by category:** More useful is to keep a record of the number of visitors by category, including passers-by. This will help you understand whether this was the right show for you to be at. Usually the majority of visitors will fall into 'contacts' with the minority in 'leads' but if you find you have very high numbers in 'passers-by' it could be the wrong show for you (don't be disheartened, it can sometimes be trial and error, and sales managers can be very convincing). If it works the other way and you have significantly high numbers in the 'prospects' and 'leads' categories, it might be worth thinking about a bigger stand, more people and more investment for the following year.

- **Pre-show marketing:** Keeping track of the direct engagements you made prior to the show opening versus the number that actually visited the stand will tell you how effective your pre-show comms plan was and also how important the show is to your target audience. If you identified and invited a number of high-profile prospects but they didn't even attend, you may question whether this trade show was the right one for you or indeed if trade shows overall are an effective tactic for networking in your industry.

- **Budget:** You can only determine if you have made a solid return on your investment if you know what your investment was. Tracking your budget throughout the whole process will help to keep you on course and minimise the risk of overspending, but in the evaluation phase it's the time to be brutally honest and reconcile every penny you spent – even the bar bills!

- **Quality of leads:** How well have the squad sorted visitors in to the different categories? Were leads really leads or were they actually prospects? Were some prospects warmer than you were anticipating? Was the information that you collected the right information to enable the next stage in comms and to move visitors along the buying process? Understanding how contacts, prospects and leads are converting helps you understand how effective the squad are and how well they understand how to categorise visitors. It may also highlight any requirement for additional training in this area before the next event.

- **Revenue:** There should be a point where you can start to put some numbers on business that has been driven as a result of the show. It can be helpful to measure this at quarterly intervals, three, six, nine and 12 months after the show. Three months should be enough of a lag time for hot leads to have converted to business, but don't forget to also measure how many contacts have become prospects and prospects have become leads. Trying to evaluate revenue before three months puts pressure on the sales process and might result in leads dropping out if they think they're being rushed into a decision.

- **Trade press coverage:** As part of the planning for your trade press strategy you will have set some targets about the number of previews/reviews that feature your business, journalist interviews and share of voice, all of which can be measured accurately as the titles are published. Don't forget to measure the outcome of ongoing dialogue with trade magazines who may want to cover more about your business than just in the show review issue – this could be the direct result of contact made because of the trade show that might not emerge until months after the event.

- **Social media:** One of the most quick and easy metrics to measure! Count up how many new followers, likes, re-tweets and connections you've generated before, during and after your trade show activity. However, you'll need to have set some objectives before the show of what you're hoping to achieve to know whether your results are good or not.

- **Audience:** If you are running any demos on your stand or presenting at any of the live theatres, keep a record of the numbers of people who attended. Did you manage to grab any of these attendees for a quick audio or video vox pop?

- **Logistics:** It helps to keep a record of the number of giveaways, brochures or samples you've distributed versus the number of people your team met to help with planning for the future. How will you know if you need more or less for the next show if you don't know what you've actually given away?

- **SMART objectives:** Whatever you set right back at the beginning of the process as the objectives you were hoping to achieve.

Evaluation is a rolling process across the year as the business results are generated from leads, but there are ways you can create interim evaluations that inform meaningful decisions about future trade show activity. Calculating return on investment (ROI) can only happen after the appropriate amount of time for business to be done has lapsed and can slow down decision-making. However, return of objectives can be calculated almost immediately and can give your business an early indication of success, thus helping you to manage expectations for future evaluations.

### Return of objectives (ROO)

ROO measures how successfully you have achieved the measurable objectives that you set in the planning stages by illustrating the outputs which have been attained. The word 'of' is used instead of the more traditional 'on' (as in return *on* investment), because to evaluate these metrics more quickly you are measuring them before any return has been generated (in most instances).

For example, if you were a food producer and your SMART objectives were:

- To distribute 300 samples of your new variety of sausage.

- To meet the buyers at Shop With Us and Better Banger and arrange a follow-up meeting.

- To hand out 150 leaflets to independent retailers who might be interested in stocking your products.

- To get mentioned in the *What's Great in Retail* show review with at least the same coverage as your main competitor.

During the show you achieved the following results with the percentage achievement of the objective given in brackets:

- Distributed 390 samples (**+30%**)
- Agreed a meeting with the buyer at Shop With Us but didn't meet Mr Better Banger (**–50%**)
- Handed out 400 leaflets to retailers (**+166%**)
- Featured in *What's Great in Retail* with exactly the same coverage as your competitor (**100%**)

This type of evaluation starts to give some numbers to demonstrate how successful your trade show execution has been. It will no doubt throw up some further questions, such as were all 400 leaflets distributed to the right retailers who have the potential to stock your sausage, and why didn't Mr Better Banger make an appearance – was he even at the show? Thankfully, because you've completed a thorough feedback process you'll have the answers to these questions and will be able to add some context to the numbers for anyone requesting them.

### Cost of objective (COO)

Measuring objectives in this way also enables you to start assigning a cost to visitors to understand how your investment fares compared to other sales tactics. For example, if you spent £7,500 overall on your entire execution, and you know you spoke with 300 people, you can calculate the cost per contact at £25. This creates the opportunity to compare with direct marketing or television where you would equally be able to work out the cost per recipient or cost per view. There may be an argument that not all 300 people you spoke to are relevant and potential buyers but is everyone who watches your TV advert going to be in your target market? None of these calculations gives a comprehensive and wholly accurate measurement (like any statistical data), but it can provide some measurable facts that are the basis for a more informed debate about the success, or otherwise of a trade show. For so long the criticism has been that trade shows are a money pit because you can't measure them and it will always be difficult because of the many variables (as with any other marketing tactic) but so long as you have some SMART objectives you can establish the value of some returns.

### Return on investment (ROI)

*When you say ROI, do you man Return on Investment or*
*Risk Of Inaction?*
—Paul Gillin, B2B social marketing strategist

The panacea of measurement for any marketing investment and undoubtedly the one that, while most often believed, is the most open to interpretation. ROI is possible for trade shows in its most basic of forms but gives little information about the what, why or how successful the trade show execution actually was. It may provide the evidence for a 'yes/no' decision on future investment in trade shows but lacks any real comprehension of whether that's the right decision or not.

The basic ROI calculation is as follows:

*Total Business Generated / Total Budget*

For example: if the total budget spent was £7,500 and total business generated from visitors to the show is £25,000, the ROI calculation is £25,000 / £7,500 so the ROI is 3:1. That is for every £1 invested in the show, £3.33 in sales has been generated.

That looks like a healthy equation for any finance director, but it also raises a number of other crucial questions such as whether that business was generated by the show in isolation or whether other marketing initiatives such as trade press and/ or advertising have also contributed to the buying decision. Also, it doesn't take into account any of the post-show costs such as sales force follow-up, which may have contributed to converting the lead and would increase the total investment. Equally, the ROI calculation doesn't take account of any business that is still in the process of conversion (which on high-value items could be two years away), or for buyers who may have bought through a third party or distributor whose sales can't be directly connected to the return figure but may have been influenced by what they saw at the show.

Repeat exhibitors who have historical data relating to the conversion rates at previous shows may be able to work out a version of ROI based on an equation of:

*Sales Revenue Potential / Total Spend*

This equation in theory will take into account the long conversion rates associated with big ticket purchases/deals that may take 12–24 months to come to fruition. For example, if from previous events you know that leads have generated approximately £10,000 in sales each within six months, you can calculate that the seven leads you have established at the show will generate roughly £70,000 of sales within six months.

ROI will always be a metric which is important to any stakeholders involved in making decisions about future trade show investment because it's familiar to them and easy to understand. However, it won't ever give a full picture of what actually happened or wholly reflect the effort and achievements that come from a trade show. So, while it will no doubt continue to be part of the evaluation conversation, make sure your stakeholders are hearing from a number of different voices that can all add value to the debate. If you find yourself having to 'justify' the future of your events, it may be worthwhile suggesting that traditionally trade shows were seen as a standalone cost in terms of marketing. However, they should be seen as an integral component of a strategic marking mix, delivering a crucial face to face element without which the effectiveness of all other marketing tactics are diluted.

The above demonstrates the rolling nature of evaluation from the day the show closes to up to 12 months afterwards to generate meaningful findings. The diagram below shows how you might plot the evaluation process and when to make decisions about booking the next event:

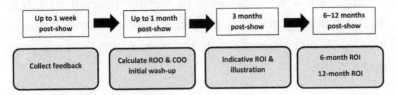

 *Return-on-investment metrics are used by 62 per cent of exhibitors, with the most popular metrics being sales revenue to cost of exhibiting (45 per cent) and sales revenue potential to cost of exhibiting (43 per cent).*
(Gardiner, 2005)

## Summary

*Study the past if you would define the future.*
—Confucius, Chinese philosopher

Well you've made it to the end and you've hopefully picked up some hints, tips and inspiration that will help you run more effective trade show campaigns long into the future. We started this chapter by emphasising how important it is to follow up and evaluate – only by doing these two things will you have any sense of how effective all the time, effort and resource you have put in has been in meeting your objectives and growing sales. Trade shows are such easy targets for criticism with a perceived lack of any measurable outcome or return and for years exhibitors haven't done much to dispel this myth. However, you're now armed with the tools, skills and confidence to demonstrate how much value your trade events are contributing to the delivery of an aligned marketing strategy.

Here are a few questions to remind yourself of things to think about from this chapter before we move onto the looking at international events and maximising the trade press opportunity.

- Have you got sufficient squad members available after the show to ensure your kit and collateral is safe during breakdown?

- Where is your kit and collateral going after the show, how is getting there and how long is it being stored?

- Who is responsible for collating and following up leads and when and how will they do it?

- Have you developed a differentiated contact strategy for contacts, prospects and leads?

- How will you move prospects along the buying journey to become leads?

- How will you ensure that you don't fall off a lead's radar – how will you keep adding value while they make a buying decision?

- What could you do creatively with leads that will surprise and delight them and help build your relationship?

- Which groups of people are you going to follow up with for feedback and what do you want to know?

- What do you need to measure to calculate ROO, COO and ROI for your event?

A huge well done – you've planned, implemented and evaluated a fantastic trade show campaign that's certain to bring incremental sales and profit to your business alongside cementing your own perception as a true event ninja. Now all you have to do is learn what you do better next year and go right back to Chapter 1 for a refresher on planning with finesse. Across the remaining pages we're going to be focusing on a couple of areas that help consolidate and amplify your trade show investment for even great success, namely managing the media and going global – it's going to be so easy after what you've just accomplished!

PART III

# FINAL CONSIDERATIONS

# CHAPTER 6

# MAXIMISING THE MEDIA

*There are only two forces that can carry light to all the corners of the globe... the sun in the heavens and the Associated Press down here.*

—Mark Twain, courtesy of the University of Iowa

Trade, consumer and social media can play a hugely influential role before, during and after your trade event not only in influencing visitors to come to your stand, but also in driving awareness of your product or service beyond attendees at the show. Depending on the resource available within your organisation there may be a communications team that are used to dealing with the media and can help you engage with them to drive your message. If it's down to you, journalists will still want to hear from and help you if you have relevant and engaging content to share with their readers.

Before you start to plan what your trade communications strategy might look like, have a think about how you will balance bought and earned media to ensure you're driving awareness and depth.

- **Bought:** Advertising space bought in the pages of magazines, or on digital platforms where you will be fully in control of the design, message and content. Usually managed by the sales/commercial teams at a magazine.

- **Earned:** You supply content to a journalist with the intention that they will cover it in relevant features, show previews/ reviews or news pieces they are writing. A journalist will write it up as they think appropriate and may not cover all the aspects you include in your release and may alter the context.

From a reader perspective, bought media works well to drive brand awareness or announce a new product or variety but will be a reasonably shallow message. Earned media can speak in much more detail about the features, benefits and advocacy of your product or service and is on average more trusted than an advert as it is seen as more impartial coming from an independent journalist. The question is often asked as to whether investment in bought drives coverage in earned and it is a grey area. A well-written, relevant and engaging press release will get picked up regardless of any investment. However, many trade magazines are free to the reader so rely on advertising for their total income – investing certainly isn't going to harm your chances of coverage, but it shouldn't be an excuse for you to submit badly written copy that isn't going to see the light of day and then question why it's not in print.

## Pre-show activity

Planning your media engagement starts long before the show opens, especially if your objective is to use the media to drive traffic to your stand. As with any aspect of trade show planning, research and objective setting are crucial for delivering an effective trade media campaign.

- **Research:** If you're new to working with the trade media, research the titles that are most appropriate to your industry and are likely to be attending the show. Event organisers may have a specific media partner which should provide a good starting point but if not, research the titles that have previously covered the event. Include reviewing the style and audience of different titles as part of your research to understand how you might need to tailor the content of your releases to appeal to different readers along with noting the frequency and format of issues (e.g., online or printed). During this process identify if any of the titles are running specific show previews that you are targeting for inclusion, or relevant product features that you could be part of in the run-up to the show. Trade magazines often have long lead times, so you would be looking to submit your content around six weeks prior to the publication date. Keep a record of the editors or key journalists and their contact details as you may want to personally invite them to your stand as the show gets closer. While we have focused mainly on trade press here as the most obvious target, don't forget bloggers, consumer press, digital platforms and any other media commentators who may be involved in covering the event and can talk to your audience on your behalf. If your time is limited, in order to give this the effort it requires seek help from an agency or a freelancer who has the knowledge and the expertise in writing this type of copy and the relationships with the magazines that they can leverage on your behalf.

- **Objectives:** To measure the effectiveness of your media campaign, setting SMART objectives as part of your planning process will help you. This could mean calculating the amount of coverage you generate, i.e., feature in three key show previews/reviews or an interview with a key member of your senior team. Alternatively, it could be targeting a number of journalists who you want to visit your stand and then tracking whether they do. If you have negotiated feature on the live theatre programme you could include an objective for the number of journalists that attend and report on that session. Whatever the appropriate metric is for you, having a SMART objective ensures that you have a tangible output to measure as part of your evaluation.

Once you have identified the key media contacts you're wanting to engage with and what your objectives are it's time to start building your engagement strategy – but you might be asking yourself whether you've anything of value they want to report on. The answer is usually an overwhelming yes, the simple fact you're exhibiting at a key industry event means you have an interest in the sector and a story to tell, so presented in an engaging and concise way, a journalist will always welcome hearing from you. There are a number of areas that could be interesting to a journalist relating to your presence at the show, which could include a new product launch, release of new consumer insight or trends, announcement of a key white paper, corporate or social responsibility news (such as job creation) and thought leadership. There should always be something of interest that you're featuring at a show that has a relevant angle for the readers of your industry's key titles. Once you've decided what you want to talk about, how do you engage with the press to inspire them to cover your story?

- **Get on their radar early:** As we've mentioned, journalists are busy people and start planning early, so engage with them at least 6–8 weeks out initially to make them aware you'll be exhibiting at the show and share brief, top-line details on what your key focus at the show will be.

- **Keep engaged:** Without being a nuisance, keep reminding journalists of what you're doing at the show and how their readers can benefit from visiting you. Most trade media platforms will have their own social media channels so join the conversation when they're talking about the show. Try and book appointments with journalists aligned to your key objectives, invite them to meet a specific member of your team and clearly articulate why they will benefit from the meeting. And always get in touch by text, email or social media on the day of the show to remind them why they should pay you a visit. As with all your other plans for the trade show, ground your communication with the media in the benefits for them and their audience – they won't visit you because you think you're great, there has to be a compelling reason why they visit you and not your competitors.

- **Contribute:** Most titles will run trade show previews and reviews so find out when they are and make sure your get your press releases, images and any product samples submitted in good time so they can include you in their content. Keep your releases short, to the point, relevant to the readers and easy to just cut and paste into a feature (see below for further details on writing a great release). Always include your stand number and contact details in any submissions or adverts so that readers can find you if they are interested. If you have the resource, set up an 'online press room' as part of your corporate website that contains all your key releases, images, videos, case studies, white papers and downloadable content that journalists can log onto and access everything they need in one place.

- **Talk to the magazine's sales team:** A lot of exhibitors avoid magazine sales teams thinking they're going to get inundated with sales calls. There might be some, but they'll be as keen as you are for you to meet your objectives – if you grow your sales that means more money to spend on advertising in future. Sales teams really can help you achieve your objectives so don't forget them! And if you are advertising remember to put the show logo and a flash with your stand number on the advert, so readers know where to find you.

- **Personalise:** Try and find a way of engaging with each journalist in a personal way that adds value for them. For example, if you know a specific magazine runs content on leadership or is very technical do you have someone in your business who could give them an interview that would be relevant for their readers? If one of your squad is doing a presentation at a live theatre, why not send invitations inviting them along followed by drinks and networking? While a consistent release should form the core of your messaging, it will help build relationships with the media if you can demonstrate you've considered and responded to what their specific readers need.

- **Press events:** Depending on your specific objectives you may want to hold a press conference or reception. These are really valuable opportunities to ensure that the media aren't distracted by other exhibitors and focus solely on your message and proposition. These can usually be held on-site in a private room at the show venue where your team can talk in more detail about a new product or demonstrate a new process. Including drinks and canapes will always make the event more attractive and sending personal invitations to the key journalists you want to show up will drive attendance. These events work well when they're kept intimate, around 12 people max, which ensures your team have time to spend with individuals following the formal presentation.

- **Call to action:** Tell the journalists what you're wanting them to do with your release. Are you looking for them to influence visitors to put you on their 'must-see' list? Or are you hoping to secure a leading profile piece for your CEO? Make it clear about how you are wanting them to help and why this would be relevant, interesting and value-adding to their readers, so journalists understand your expectations.

- **Use the organisers' collateral:** Often the show organisers will have appointed a PR company who will be sending out generic show releases before, during and after the show (details are usually in the Exhibitor Manual). Contributing to the show's own publicity is a great way of driving exposure of what you're doing and not many exhibitors usually do it. And don't forget to leave copies of your press release and samples in the organisers' press office for the press to collect.

## At the show

With a solid pre-show engagement plan you should be confident that once the show opens you'll have created the necessary engagement for the media to visit your stand and cover your story in their reviews. However, it never hurts to remind journalists of your appointment on the day with a quick 'Looking forward to speaking with you later' tweet or email. Equally, as part of your own social media planning for during the show, follow the media's accounts, contribute and be part of the conversation.

Your squad may be nervous about being approached by the media on the stand, feeling anxious that they're going to say the wrong thing and generate negative coverage. Assigning one person specifically to the role of media liaison may negate some of these concerns, but as this isn't always possible there are some key guidelines you can follow to help ensure your whole squad are able to manage conversations with the media to maximise your story.

- **Messaging:** As part of your squad training agree your concise elevator pitch and ensure everyone feels confident in articulating the same consistent objectives for the show including why visitors will benefit from talking to you. Practice this with your team until they are comfortable – without it becoming robotic. Having a USB stick (containing releases, images, case studies, contact details, etc.) ready for your squad to hand out will ensure journalists get the same information. Branded notebooks and pen are always useful giveaways for these guys.

- **Sound bites**: Prepare several different soundbites using simple, concise language (avoiding internal jargon or acronyms) that your squad feel comfortable using in response to the likely questions journalists might ask.

- **Referral:** Don't be afraid to take details and say you'll get back to them with further detail on anything you're unsure of. It's better to follow up later with the right answer as opposed to hastily supplying the wrong one, which could lead to issues later on.

- **Always on the record:** While it's important to be friendly and helpful with the media, avoid becoming too relaxed or complacent, there isn't really any such thing as 'off the record'. Work on the premise that if you don't want to see it in print, don't say it. If you are giving some background knowledge to the media, ensure that they know it's not attributable before saying something. There is no taking something back once it's been said and unfortunately it could still be attributed to you. Unless you have proof to the contrary (and deep pockets) to take your grievance any further you've got to live with the end result.

*Loose lips may sink ships.*

—WWII Slogan Campaign by the US War Advertising Council – courtesy Ad. Council Archives, University of Illinois Archives, RS 13/2/207

- **Flip it:** Sometimes journalists may ask a difficult question looking for a specific angle that may not be positive. In this situation, avoid repeating any negative statements made by the journalist and flip it around for a more positive response. For example, when introducing a new limited-edition flavour of your product, a journalist might ask 'Is the only reason you're introducing this as a limited-edition because you're not sure whether your consumers will like it or not?'. That may very well be the reason but the answer shouldn't be: 'That's absolutely correct, we're not sure if consumers will like it so we're going to give it a try and see what happens.' A more positive response would be: 'We know from the vast consumer research we conduct that our consumers love experimenting and trying new things, so creating limited-editions allows them to stay connected with the brand through always having something new to try.'

You and your squad may understandably be nervous about talking to the media, assuming that they will be looking to trip you up in some way. In general, trade media will always be looking for great content that is relevant for their readers and to help support suppliers in meeting their objectives. On the positive side, remember that their sales teams don't want to see you remove your advertising support for the magazine over some trivial comment and their journalist will be fully aware of this, so unless it is of major significance, you should be OK. However, if you remember that nothing is ever 'off the record' and if you don't want to see it in print, don't say it, then the media should be a hugely effective and collaborative channel to achieve your aims.

## Post-show activity

Hopefully your hard work paid off and you met some valuable media contacts at the show who will be able to help tell your story long after the doors close. As with anything else relating to trade shows, now's the time to follow up and ensure you share everything you committed to, but also to check that the journalists are keeping their side of the deal. Journalists will have a lot to cover from the show, so don't take it personally if they don't cover your content in the first instance but do be persistent. If you know your story is relevant and engaging, and the journalist seemed to agree with you, keep checking in with them to confirm when they'll be covering it. It may be that they are keeping it for an upcoming feature which they think will be more relevant or hoping to run it at the same time as an interview with your MD that you agreed at the show.

Aside from just following up on the contact you made at the show there are other ways in which you can engage with the media to prolong the life of your investment in the show:

- **Blog guest contributor:** Ask a journalist to create a guest blog for your website featuring their highlights from the show and the key things they learned. For your audience this builds your credibility and for the journalist it might expose them to a new audience within your industry.

- **Highlights release:** Circulate your own release covering the key outputs from the show, mentioning the contacts you met and insight of interest from the key speaker sessions. Remember to set this in the context of relevance for a magazine's readers – they're probably not that interested in the fact you met 700 people, but they might want to know that your product is now available for them to buy from their local wholesaler, or that a complementary supplier released a fantastic new labour-saving product.

- **Outcomes release:** If your presence at the show leads to any additional success such as winning an industry award, setting up a new apprentice scheme or winning new export business, even if it's months after the show, it is still worth sharing the news with the media where it's relevant to their readers.

- **Keep in touch:** If you're going to invest in the show again next year you're likely to target the same media titles, hence keeping in touch with the contacts you've made will make your job easier in the future. If you've kept in touch across the year, it's likely that a journalist will already have you on their radar when planning the next show preview.

- **Senior profile:** As you build trust and relationships with the media, there may be opportunities to extend your coverage beyond simple news releases and develop deeper contact such as interviews with your senior team and thought leadership pieces. This will help to broaden your organisation's appeal as a category authority beyond just the audience at the show.

Assuming you've set objectives for the amount of coverage you were hoping to generate through your media activity, you should be able to measure your results soon after the show closes. There is much debate about how to measure press activity and it can be as simple as counting the number of pieces of coverage you were hoping to achieve versus the number actually delivered. Some businesses count the number of words talking about their organisation versus a competitor (share of voice), the column inches or whether quotes and images are included. However, a concise, impactful value-adding comment can be more powerful with readers than pages of content that doesn't inspire or inform.

## Writing great content

Basically, driving great content through the media, whether related to a trade show or not is all about supplying interesting, engaging and relevant content that both the journalist and the reader gets value from. The more you can use your story to show a potential customer how your product or service can help solve their problem, the more likely you are to generate coverage. Creating content isn't about selling your product or broadcasting the features, it's about using a number of media tactics such as written, video, images and audio to share knowledge and expertise that builds trust with your audience. At a B2B level, much media content will be through written press releases, so here are some quick tips to help in drafting your pre-show, during and post-show releases:

- **Headline:** A succinct overview of the content stating the what, where, why, who and when relating to the show. For example, a Yorkshire coffee roaster might use the headline 'Yorkie Roast *(who)* planning to brew up success for coffee retailers *(what and why)* at Business Yorkshire *(where)* in August *(when)*'. The headline should entice a reader to keep reading, articulate who is doing what and why it is relevant for visitors. The first line should be a seamless continuation of the headline so in this instance, 'New coffee roaster Yorkie Roast is targeting independent coffee shop owners at next month's Business Yorkshire event with a special promotional deal on their unique coffee pods which deliver superior taste for coffee-lovers and enhanced profits for retailers.'

- **Tell all in the first paragraph:** Don't hide the story at the bottom of the page; get to the point quickly. You might think you're building anticipation and taking the reader through the context of your story but in reality, if you don't get to the good bit until the end, you'll have lost them!

- **Show don't tell:** As with everything, ground your content in how it benefits the reader and the wider audience. Stick to one key message about how a visitor will benefit from coming to your stand and show the ways in which you'll add value to their day and decision-making.

- **Keep it simple:** Use simple, direct and jargon-free language (unless it's commonly understood throughout your industry), and when you mention features of your product or service be sure to convert this to benefits for the buyer.

- **Quotes:** Break up the static text by using quotes from members of your team but try to stick to the same person to avoid confusing your audience.

- **Mixed media:** Use a range of media to accompany your release – good high-res images are a necessity, but if you have any video or audio this can disrupt and catch the attention of a reader in a more engaging way. Especially in the post-show release, images or video showing the highlights of your stand in operation and the numbers of visitors supports your claim of how successful your show was. While videos won't appear in print, most titles these days have a digital presence and could use your video on their website or social media. On average a release accompanied by a video is three times more likely to be covered.

- **Call to action:** Ensure the reader knows what you want them to do next and give them the details to do it. For example, if you're using the media to drive traffic to your stand, offer an incentive or free gift exclusively to the magazine's readers that can be claimed at the stand but make sure they know how to do that, i.e., bring a copy of the magazine or use a code word for redemption. In post-show coverage, if you're looking to influence readers to download a white paper you launched at the show, make sure they know where to download or request it. And always include contact details for anyone wanting more information.

- **Timely:** Journalists are busy people and constantly being inundated with press releases and content. Be respectful of their time, making their job as easy as you possibly can by hitting their deadlines and following through on any promises made.

## Summary

Trade media can be an extremely powerful medium through which to share the message about your participation in the show not just with visitors but with the wider industry audience. Recognised as a credible, impartial and knowledgeable voice, trade media is more likely to influence and engage with your audience than a number of your own direct marketing initiatives. By developing powerful messaging, initiating discussions and building relationships with the key influencers within your industry's media, you will ensure that your story is heard and acted upon to the widest possible audience.

To help you plan and execute your media strategy ask yourself:

- Which are the priority titles in the market that you want to engage with?

- What do you want journalists to cover and why is this relevant to their readers?

- Have you developed a strategic plan for pre-show, during and post-show media activity?

- How will you align earned and bought media? What budget is available for advertising?

- How will you add value for journalists beyond just a press release?

- Who is responsible for delivering the media contact strategy for your trade show campaign?

- How comfortable are your squad in dealing with the media and what additional support and/or training might they need?

- Which multimedia content options do you have available such as images and video?

- How will you ensure that your content gets covered?

- How will you measure the success of your media strategy?

- Do you need some external support to ensure you are maximising the opportunities that may present?

*Trade isn't about goods. Trade is about information.*
*Goods sit in the warehouse until information moves them.*
—C.J. Cherryh, Chanur's Legacy

Now you've nailed this exhibition thing, let's go global in the next (and final!) chapter.

# CHAPTER 7

# GOING GLOBAL

*A journey of a thousand miles, begins with a single step.*
—Lao Tuz, ancient Chinese philosopher and writer

Now you've developed a strong business and exhibited at your first domestic trade show your thoughts may be turning to the potential and glamour of international markets. You'll notice we've qualified the last sentence by suggesting you have already executed a show in your home market. We feel it's crucial in ensuring success when planning a global campaign to make your mistakes at homes first (there will always be some). Unless you really have absolutely no option, we'd strongly advise only investing in international shows when you have at least one domestic event under your belt. Any mistakes will be easier and cheaper to rectify at home than they will ever be abroad and until you fully appreciate how customers are reacting to your product in your own language you've little hope of understanding it in a foreign one.

However, once you've nailed your first event and are thinking about the potential of international shows, you'll find that many of the principles of the P.I.E. process are exactly the same with a few additional considerations around logistics, language and culture.

## Which show?

Exporting can introduce your product or service to higher numbers of new prospects and leads, expand your footprint, grow sales and profits and develop internal capability. On the flip side, it can also increase risk and cash-flow exposure, generate more paperwork and bring unexpected anxiety in understanding the market and trading patterns of unknown audiences. However, with careful planning, consideration and advice from the experts it can be a lucrative and exciting channel to develop.

With 31,000 certified trade shows globally every year, how do you choose which is the right one for your business? (UFI, 2014). Deciding which market and trade show to attend is much the same process as it would be for a domestic event and it all comes down to research. Here are some of the elements to consider when selecting whether an international show is right for you and which one to attend:

- **Market:** If you assume that the majority of visitors to a show will be from the domestic market or surrounding countries are you confident that your proposition has potential in that market? Different markets are at different states of readiness and what customers are ready for at home may be very different from the stage an overseas market is at. Equally, your proposition may be at the end of its life stage in the market you're intending to exhibit at. Just because there is an 'industry' show for your sector in a country don't assume that by default the visitors to it will be in the right position to buy your product.

- **Route to market:** How will you service the market if you are successful in generating orders? There would be nothing worse than investing in a trade show where your product was well received, with orders generated only to find that you can't physically supply customers. Equally, be clear about what you're looking for from an international show – is it direct customers, a distributor, sales agent or manufacturing partner? Being clear about who you need to meet to supply the market will help with filtering out the passers-by who can't add any value to achieving your objectives.

- **Resource:** If you thought domestic trade shows were expensive, wait until you try and fund an international one, which can require almost three times the budget on average. In fact, industry research suggests that exhibiting in the US is on average five times more expensive than in Europe (Bonnaud, 2016). The cost of logistics, transport, amends to your stand, accommodation, translators, local experts, local fees and everything else needed can rack up thousands in additional costs. Not only will significantly more budget be required but it will take more time to plan an international trade show when you consider moving kit and people to the right venue, briefing and managing translators and following up to a more dispersed audience. International trade shows can be a profitable stream of new business, but they will require a considerable investment up front.

- **Competition:** Your brand is likely to have low awareness in a new international market and there could be experienced competitors who are already doing a good job. In this instance are you certain that your product has enough differentiation to appeal to customers in an international market? Your product or service may have been first to market in your domestic environment but that doesn't necessarily mean this will be the case in foreign markets and your competition could already be much better known and doing a good job – making it expensive and time-consuming for you to cut through and achieve success.

*The top two criteria cited most often when selecting a foreign event are:*
1. *Attendee demographics: 65%*
2. *Geographical regions served: 44%*
(*Skyline, 2008*)

If you've considered all these elements and are confident that exhibiting at an international event will give you the catalyst for growth that you want, everything you have already learnt in this book will help you plan, execute and evaluate a successful campaign. However, there are three main elements that require more careful consideration as part of your planning, namely logistics, language and culture.

## Logistics

Everything about getting your kit and people to an international show will be that bit more complicated, not impossible but definitely requiring more thought and consideration. The distance between your base and event market will determine how much more time you need to add into your planning but essentially the earlier you can start the better, and the cheaper it will be. If you're planning on having a very small space with minimal kit the planning will be much less complex but if you're taking any kind of samples, products or unusual items beware of the international regulations regarding entry to the country you'll be exhibiting in as well as any countries your goods may have to travel via. There are a number of variables such as bad weather, international bank holidays and cargo checking that can all impact on your timescale over which you have absolutely no control, hence the more time you give yourself, the lower the risk of these impacting on your delivery.

There's a really easy route to making the whole logistics process as smooth as possible and that's to use the official freight forwarders as nominated by the show organisers (details of which will be found in the Exhibitor Manual). There's good reason why the event organisers have selected them (because they're excellent at what they do) and while they may seem more expensive than other independent suppliers, we've heard far more horror stories of disaster than we have of success using the non-appointed forwarders. Freight forwarders will be experts in understanding the logistics of the venue and the show, such as build-up and breakdown times and access, while also having good relationships with local ports, entry points and carriers. Freight forwarders will also be able to help you with several different elements of your planning including:

- **Costs:** Advising on what you need to budget for to fund port charges, consular fees, insurance, freight handling, carrier costs, etc.

- **Cargo method:** Advising you on the most effective methods of transporting your kit and goods, e.g., land, sea, air and also negotiating space and costs with carriers on your behalf. Sea freight will almost always be cheaper than air freight but takes a lot longer, which is where early planning is crucial to avoid limiting your transport options or breaking your budgetary constraints.

- **Paperwork:** Helping you understand what paperwork needs to be completed to ensure your kit and goods are allowed to travel and enter into the country and how to complete it accurately. They will also ensure you know where it needs to be submitted and by when, so you don't miss any crucial deadlines.

- **Customs brokers:** Ensuring that everything you're supplying for the show complies with local customs regulations and highlighting any areas of sensitivity that may require additional information or require attention to detail (even concerning countries you are travelling through to your ultimate destination).

In case we haven't mentioned it before, it's advisable to use the organisers' freight forwarders if you're shipping anything more complicated than yourself and a couple of brochures. It will inevitably save you time, money and stress to employ the experts to get your kit to the right place on time. Equally, if anything does go wrong and you need some help, the organisers are much more likely to help you and put pressure on the freight forwarders to find a solution if you're using the organisation they've recommended.

However, many exhibitors have sourced third-party logistics suppliers and built strong, collaborative relationships that have produced good results. If you think you're able to manage the freight forwarder yourself and want to select your own supplier here are some areas to consider when choosing who to work with:

- Ensure they have an office close to the exhibition venue and the port you're shipping to – being hundreds of miles away is not going to help if any problems arise.

- Confirm they have experience working with your product and understand the local rules and regulations relating to your specific sector.

- Make sure they are financially stable and have a good credit rating so that your goods are not at risk in their possession.

- Ask existing customers for testimonials and reviews to understand how satisfied they are with levels of service. Also check their relationships and reputation with carriers to identify any issues or concerns.

- Compare the shipping rates of a few different suppliers to ensure you're getting the best value – this doesn't mean the cheapest quote but understand exactly what you can expect for your money (and be suspicious of very low-cost quotes).

- Check their services will transport your goods from the port to the exhibition venue – some don't quote fees for onward transport in initial costs.

- Check their membership of trade associations and ensure they are bonded and licensed by the relevant authorities.

Getting yourself, your kit, your product and equipment to the right place at the right time will be one of the biggest differences you will encounter in moving from a domestic to international show and unless you're a logistics company, employing the recognised experts will always give you the best chance of success.

There is one consideration that may cut your costs of exhibiting abroad – build and/or store your stand near to the event space instead of shipping your domestic stand half way around the world and back or simply hire a generic stand that you can customise instead and reduce your carbon footprint in doing so!

If you need to take your own stand, maybe you ship it to a number of foreign locations across the year, work with your stand provider to ensure you are using the lightest and therefore the most cost-effective materials you can according to your budget. What you may pay up-front for a top-notch stand may save you a heap of money with the reduction in freight costs due to the reduction in the stand's weight and increased ability to be more compactable in transit.

## Language

*We cannot always oblige, but we can always speak obligingly.*

—Voltaire (François-Marie Arouet), French Enlightenment writer, historian and philosopher

It's often said that English is the international language of business and you will often find that English is the language predominantly spoken at international events, but to think it's the only language that matters is disrespectful to the market you're visiting. If nothing else, learning a couple of phrases of welcome, thanks and goodbye will show visitors that you have at least made the effort to try and engage with them on a more personal level. The question of whether you will need to employ native speakers on your stand and translate your literature will depend on a number of factors, including which market you're exhibiting in, how complex your product and message is and the sophistication of visitors to the show. For example, the needs would be very different for a multinational car manufacturing show held in Hannover, to a small, regional food fair held in a rural part of India.

You will undoubtedly find that you're even more inundated with offers to help on the stand when you announce that you're planning on exhibiting in a foreign market and this is where your skills in selecting the most effective squad will be valuable. Many exhibitors have the perception that they're on holiday when exhibiting internationally and that the usual rules of what's acceptable don't apply. International events can be even more exhausting than domestic ones, having experienced a long and tiring journey, having to concentrate harder to understand accents when speaking with visitors and not being surrounded by the usual home comforts. International exhibitions are not about open-top bus tours and fine dining – if you see more than the event venue and your hotel you're probably doing something wrong. So select your squad carefully and it may be worth considering employing the services of a native speaker to act as the host on your stand, making introductions to visitors and understanding their level of need before passing them onto members of your own team. If you can engage a host who can speak several languages that will be relevant, this is even more valuable. If you have existing business in the market, consider inviting customers or your distributor/agent to attend the show with you to act as an initial point of contact with visitors.

When you are speaking in English to visitors at international events (or even international visitors at your domestic events), build your relationship by giving them space and time to understand what you're saying without making them feel pressurised or stupid. Speak slowly, clearly and using simple (non-technical) language. Try to keep sentences short and to the point – one message or idea only per sentence, leaving them plenty of time to comprehend what you've said and form a response. And be really sure about jokes, acronyms and idioms before you use them – suggesting to a potential customer that the 'ball is in their court' or that your product is 'the best thing since sliced bread' is unlikely to do much for building their trust or demonstrating your expertise.

The most efficient way to execute your stand will be to use your existing collateral such as stand graphics and literature, but before you simply pack up your current brochures think about the messaging and context. Would the wording on your collateral have the same meaning in the market you're visiting, or would it need further explanation? Is the problem being solved the same as in your domestic market, or is it something slightly different in the global context? Often exhibitors just transfer exactly the same proposition to international markets without thinking about how that will be perceived and understood. Think about how you might need to change the messaging (not the proposition) to ensure that visitors from an international market would understand your product or service in their own context. In addition to this, be aware of talking the same language in terms of measurements and dimensions – countries may use different units (e.g., centimetres versus inches), which has been the downfall of many exhibitors who have arrived on-site only to realise their kit doesn't fit the space they'd booked (particularly poignant when exhibiting in the USA where their booths are usually measured imperially rather than metrically).

*Businesses which are proactive in their use of foreign languages achieve on average 4X more export sales – ELAN: Effects on the European economy of shortages of foreign language skills in enterprise.*
(CiLT, 2006)

Whether you need to translate your literature will depend on the market you're visiting and the complexity of your message, but if you have the budget it is only ever going to add value to your offer and help to build relationships. However, this is another area where you shouldn't try to save money by doing it yourself (unless you're a native speaker) and automated, online translate is definitely not the answer. Employing a translator ensures that you maintain a professional appearance and avoids any embarrassing mistakes. If you have a highly technical product with lots of detail in your literature, it's worth ensuring that your translator has experience in this sector and understands what you're trying to communicate to the specific audience. Translators usually work on a cost per word basis, so only convert the minimum required to get your message across to avoid spending unnecessary budget. Employing a translator as early in the planning as possible means you're leaving plenty of time for them to sense-check messaging and complete a full proofread. As part of your agreement they should allow you to send the translation on to someone you know who is able to read it and check it out for you before you pay for the service. When you have agreed the translation, one final check of the laid-out literature by your translator is essential (which again you should negotiate as part of their overall service). Designers can often leave out crucial symbols or punctuation, thinking them irrelevant, which completely changes the meaning of the text.

Language could be one on the key barriers between you and your prospective customer making a connection, so if you're anticipating that a particular market is going to play a significant role in your future expansion, learning some of the basics isn't going to do any harm. As with any aspect of trade show execution, it will always be worth investing the budget to employ the experts who can ensure that you deliver a meaningful and value-adding proposition for visitors that generates profitable sales. Never rely on your prospective customer's translator alone, especially if you get into negotiations over quantities and price, you need your own reputable translation.

 *Seventy-nine per cent of exhibitors employ multilingual squad members at overseas trade events.*
(Skyline, 2008)

## Culture

The other key aspects to consider as part of your planning are the local customs and traditions that are relevant to the market in which you're looking to operate. There will be clearly defined 'dos and don'ts' in doing business in different markets and ignorance of these could cost you dearly. The event organisers should be able to provide clear guidance on local customs, as will the relevant trade association in the country. It is worth investing time to understand the process and decision-making for business decisions in the market you're looking to enter as this will help you plan the resource required for follow-up and conversions. For example, if there is traditionally a very long conversion process based on several face-to-face meetings, the budget required to follow this up may be significant, with any return measured in months or years versus weeks. Equally, there may be some markets where visitors are highly digitally engaged, making quick purchase decisions based on remote and digital touchpoints (e.g., email and Skype).

Aside from business customs and traditions, there may be a number of more general country-based traditions that it will be important to observe. For example, in China, it is customary that the eldest in a group is greeted first, while in India it could cause offence to touch someone's head so try to avoid this (unless you're selling hats!). Researching the local customs and traditions is crucial in ensuring that you don't cause any offence before you've even had the opportunity to start a relationship. While some traditions and customs may seem strange and unnecessary to you, don't ignore them as they will be meaningful to your visitors and showing respect for them is one of the easiest ways to build trust with new contacts. Also consider whether the colours you're using in your collateral or gifts you're giving away are likely to cause any offence. For example, in Mexico avoid using red flowers in your graphics or as a giveaway (especially marigolds) as they have a negative connotation, even representing death. While in the UAE anything relating to alcohol, dogs, pork or knives (a symbol of severing ties) should be avoided as a gift, as should clocks, watches and handkerchiefs in China as this could be taken as you are wishing their life away! To the Japanese, gift-giving shows respect, friendship and appreciation and is a centuries-old ritual with a host of associated protocol that you get wrong at your peril.

Aside from general behaviour and customs, familiarise yourself with the more conventional rules of operation in the country, e.g., cash versus credit cards, tipping, transport, bank opening times, etc., to ensure that you know how to deal with any situations and problems that might arise while you're visiting. It's also worth taking advice on the acceptable dress code both for the market and the industry you're operating in and respecting it. Even if your preferred uniform is branded polo shirts, if formal business dress is the norm in your target market then it is advisable for your squad to reflect this. Finally, understanding what is acceptable in terms of post-show entertainment and hospitality is worth researching to ensure you don't offend anyone by suggesting a venue or activity that would cause offence, or not inviting a spouse or family if this expected.

You're likely to be investing significantly more budget in an international event so the final point to emphasise is how hard your pre-show marketing will have to work to drive a return. An international show has the potential to attract up to three to four times more visitors than the domestic show you're used to and therefore prospects are even less likely to find you by chance. Making appointments with key distributors and prospects and engaging with key contacts to get on their must-see list before they arrive will be more important than ever – and needs to start early.

Don't underestimate the benefits and potential pitfalls of not researching the culture of the market you want to penetrate properly. When you start to research your target market the following considerations might be helpful:

- What are the necessary social and business protocols that you and your squad will need to observe at all times? Greetings and goodbyes, religion, gender roles, appearance, consumption of food and drink – all of which may be slightly different when interacting in a business or in a social environment. Inviting a business contact to a social event without their family or partner could be a faux pas in some societies! Many cultures have strict protocols when it comes to meetings, e.g., who sits where, how the meetings are conducted and the types of presentations to share and when. Many cultures will decline a gift offered to them out of politeness a few times before actually accepting it (a practice you need to follow if offered a gift yourself) and in China, for instance, small trinkets are exchanged rather than expensive gifts which may embarrass the recipient. The one area you may definitively require expert advice on could be around ethical standards and the degree of corruption in certain countries and how you need to deal with this without falling foul of the authorities there and back home.

- What are the underpinning dos and don'ts when communicating and interacting with this audience both in person and digitally? Avoid causing embarrassment or offence – one of the easiest pitfalls to fall into here can be around gestures, personal space, touching and facial expressions when interacting in person; a thumbs up in one country could be seen as an insult in another. In some countries it is offensive to open up a gift that has been presented to you unless you are asked to, you should open it in private.

- Are you able to identify any mutual similarities in culture that you can use in conversation to start to develop a favourable interaction with your customers? Topics could include sport, art, music, food, etc., anything that can give you a passive conversational piece but avoid topics that could cause offence such as religion and politics and be careful with humour, what you find funny may cause offense elsewhere.

- Do they have any stereotypical ideas about your culture that you may have to overcome or avoid? If presented with an observation that you don't appear to fit their idea of a typical region just smile and laugh it off, don't take or show offence, if you feel it is required have a stock response prepared for your squad to reply with that doesn't equally cause offence to the recipient.

- Are there any stereotypical notions about their culture that your squad need to be aware about and avoid at all costs?

- Research any events and trends that are currently impacting the target culture as this may give you a conversational in or at least an indication that this is the right market for your product at this time – again religion and politics should be off the list of topics to explore as conversation openers but consider topics such as technology, a change in dominant industries, standard of living, access to education, and the natural environment. The religious and political situation should be considered to ensure you're not entering into a market that could dramatically change for the worse due to potential events and should be part of your overall review of the viability of the market.

- Do you have shared history that could be of interest and that could be exploited to your advantage? Is there anything in your mutual past that always needs to be off topic?

The best way to avoid unnecessary time and effort would be to liaise with your local government agencies who will be more than helpful in offering practical advice and signposting you to other resources that will be open to a potential exporter such as yourself. Once you have your research, share it between the squad pre-show and discuss it during your daily briefing sessions at the show to ensure it is front-of-mind for them.

*Whatever words we utter should be chosen with care, for*
*people will hear them and be influenced by them*
*for good or ill.*

—Buddha

## Summary

International events can open up an exciting, lucrative and dynamic sales opportunity for businesses, and trade shows are a valuable starting point to engage with potential new customers. However, this should only be embarked upon with the understanding that it will take time, money and effort to plan, execute and follow-up, and without experience of exhibiting in your domestic market, could create several costly pitfalls.

Depending on your domestic location there are likely to be a number of local support organisations that can help with practical advice, funding and expertise. In the UK, the Department for International Trade has a wealth of knowledge as well as a support programme that can help exhibitors navigate their first overseas trips. Often these organisations offer organised missions to specific international events, as the DIT does, or manage country pavilions where businesses can be part of a collaborative national delegation and take a space on a larger country-based stand.

So before you head off and book your plane tickets here are a few areas to consider from this chapter:

- Which markets are ready for your product or service and are you able to service it efficiently? If so, which trade shows in those markets will attract your ideal potential contacts?

- Are you looking to meet direct customers, distributors, sales agents or manufacturers?

- What additional budget would you need in terms of logistics, language and culture to execute a trade show effectively?

- How would you need to amend your stand design, graphics and literature to ensure that your proposition was understood and added value for visitors?

- Would you need to translate any of your current collateral to use it at an international show?

- Do you have the necessary resource available to follow up with contacts based on the general business process for the market?

*The world can run without money and currencies but not without business and trade.*

—Amit Kalantri, *Wealth of Words*

# CLOSING REMARKS

*A dream doesn't become reality through magic; it takes sweat, determination and hard work.*

— General Colin L. Powell USA (Ret)

Well as General Colin L. Powell so brilliantly states, your sweat, determination and hard work have transformed your trade show dreams to reality, although no doubt several of your colleagues will be thinking it all happened by magic. You know how hard you've worked in bringing your campaign to life, the decisions you've had to wrestle with, the squad members you've had to have awkward conversations with and the passers-by you've had to ruthlessly let go as they deliver no value to your business. So, before you get too heavily stuck into planning the next one, sit back, relax and revel just for a second in the brilliance of an excellently executed exhibition – well done you (and your inner magician)!

Over the last seven chapters we hope we've inspired you to find the right answers for your organisation, given you the confidence to try some new things and challenge your internal cynics and stakeholders whilst providing the roadmap to start generating profitable sales from your trade show campaigns. There aren't too many rights and wrongs in trade shows (apart from eating on your stand, that's always wrong) so we couldn't ever give you the magic recipe that guarantees success, but we have tried to help you ask yourself the right questions that give you the best chance of success. Chapter 1 might seem like a long time ago so let's go right back to the beginning and recap on the key points we've covered since page 1!

## Total recap

- Despite the growth of digital marketing, people still buy from people and are increasingly looking for deeper and more meaningful personal relationships – trade shows and exhibitions create the perfect environment for that.

- Trade shows take significant amounts of time, money, effort, people and focus – if your business doesn't have plenty of all of them then reconsider whether trade shows can be an effective tactic for you.

- Trade shows work most effectively as part of an integrated marketing plan and rarely perform strongly as an isolated tactic – ensure you have all the tools in place to amplify your trade show investment.

- There are 31,000 registered shows around the world with millions of visitors – it's worth spending the time up front to ensure you're exhibiting at the show that's most likely to bring you an audience of high value prospects.

- You can measure the commercial return of your investment in trade shows but only if you set SMART objectives and understand how and what you're going to measure as part of your planning process.

- Buying floor space and creating your stand only accounts for just over half of your budget – there are a whole range of other services, equipment and costs that you might need to fund to truly maximise your whole campaign.

- Creating an engaging stand that clearly articulates your value proposition is important – but getting your stand on a visitor's must-see list before doors open is even more important.

- The Exhibitor Manual is your best friend – read it, digest it, review it, caress it (OK, now we're getting carried away) – it is the key to ensuring all your hard work actually does come to life.

- Understanding who you're wanting to connect with and how you're going to collect the information you need to keep in touch with them is a crucial task in the planning phase – just because you get a badge-scanner free as part of your package doesn't mean you have to use it if you need more information than it can offer.

- Visitors usually need several hints before they'll decide to visit your stand – one advert in the show guide isn't going to cut it. A timely, aligned and consistent pre-show marketing campaign will help generate the right footfall to your stand.

- Choose your stand squad – don't let it choose you. Blend your squad so that you have a range of different skills and expertise that complement each other and if someone really doesn't want to be at a trade show, leave them in the office.

- You only get one chance to make a first impression, so working out your opening lines before you get on-site will give you a better chance of connecting with the people who can makes the biggest positive impact on your business.

- Your brain may be bursting with your objectives, plans and logistics for the show but if you don't share them with your squad how are they supposed to know what you want them to do? Planning a squad training session ensures you're all on the same page.

- Not every visitor is valuable for you so don't feel guilty about moving along the time-wasters. Create the filtering process that enables your squad to spend the most time with the 16–20% of visitors who can actually do business with you.

- Eighty-seven per cent of leads never get followed up – be one of the 13% club!

- Don't be too impatient with your follow-up – it can take up to seven contacts and 12 months to generate a sale from a trade show. Planning your follow-up content strategy before the show will help you get ahead of the game afterwards.

- Feedback is a gift – except when it isn't. Ask a wide variety of audiences for their thoughts (visitors, squad, exhibitors) and take what is useful to inform how you'll do it better next time.

- Try not to be too eager in calculating a return – sales can take months to convert from leads. Use ROO and COO as interim signs of the success of your trade show.

- The media can help you amplify your message beyond just the trade show audience but to get the most from them, proactively share content that adds value for their audience – and remember nothing's ever off the record.

- International trade shows are fantastic opportunities to reach new markets but they're certainly not a holiday. If you thought planning for a domestic event took time, effort and money, you'll need at least double of all three for an international event.

Phew... we got through quite a lot, didn't we? Feeling overwhelmed and slightly dazed? Don't panic, there's a lot to think about but just break it down into the bite-sized chunks we've shared in the book and take it one stage at a time. Just by picking up this book and learning from the advice and suggestions within you've already made a huge leap in ensuring your next event will be more organised, more effective and generate more sales than previous campaigns.

If you are still overwhelmed and feeling unsure, your journey doesn't have to end here. There are regular updates, blogs and new insights being shared on the www.inspiringexhibitors. com website as well as advice and support from the exhibitor community. Fortnightly podcasts are published on Podbean and iTunes featuring experts from the entire exhibition community sharing their expertise, advice and knowledge and we also answer any listener's problems through the Trade Show Trouble section. Links to the podcasts can be found on the website.

If you're still needing some more help and advice, we run regular training workshops and webinars, details of which can again be found on the website. We'd be delighted to hear from you about your specific needs, whether that's some consultancy and mentoring to help you navigate the process yourself, or if you've decided you simply don't have the resource to deliver trade shows in-house, we can take over the entire end-to-end management for you. Please drop us a line at proextra@12th-man-solutions.co.uk and we'll be happy to talk through your specific requirements.

If, however you're feeling inspired and are raring to go, then good luck with everything, we wish you a fantastically successful show, generating lots of high-potential leads that convert to profitable, long-term relationships. Please do let us know how you get on and anything new that your learned along the way. And as a final sign off, in case we forgot to mention it... don't eat on your stand!

www.inspiringexhibitors.com

# CONTACT DETAILS

## Nichola Reeder

- Email: nichola@12th-man-solutions.co.uk
- Twitter: @12th_Mans_Lady
- LinkedIn: www.linkedin.com/in/nichola-reeder-377b4826

## Steve Reeder

- Email: steve@12th-man-solutions.co.uk
- Twitter: @12thmansolution
- LinkedIn: www.linkedin.com/in/steve-reeder-4140a019

## ProExTra

- Website: www.inspiringexhibitors.com
- Email: proextra@12th-man-solutions.co.uk

## Podcasts

- iTunes: https://itunes.apple.com/gb/podcast/inspiring-exhibitors/id1437646853?mt=2
- Podbean: https://inspiringexhibitors.podbean.com
- Twitter: @ProExTraCo
- LinkedIn: www.linkedin.com/company/12th-man-solutions-limited
- YouTube: www.youtube.com/channel/UCFEkSHruqjOYIXJ--zi2ApA
- Facebook: www.facebook.com/Proextraco

## 12th Man Solutions Ltd and ProExTra are trading names of Twelfth Man Solutions Ltd

Twelfth Man Solutions Ltd is registered in England and Wales Company Number: 8450913

VAT Number: 160 8762 96

Registered Office: Sælig House, 6 Derwent Close, Redmarshall TS21 1HS

Website: www.12th-man-solutions.co.uk

LinkedIn: www.linkedin.com/company/12th-mansolutions-limited/

Email: info@12th-man-solutions.co.uk

Facebook: www.facebook.com/12thManSolutionsLtd/

## Artwork credit

The caricatures in this book were created by Darren 'Dezzy' Cairns: Dezzy@dezzydesigns.co.uk

# BIBLIOGRAPHY

Adams, C. (2012). Staff Training. Exhibitor Online. Available at: http://exhibitoronline.com/topics/article.asp?ID=1520 (Accessed 2 November 2018).

Aslam, S. (2018). Pinterest by the Numbers (2018): Stats, Demographics & Fun Facts. Omnicoreagency.com. Available at: www.omnicoreagency.com/pinterest-statistics (Accessed 14 August 2018).

Bailey, M. (2004). Marketing Your Business. Available at: www.marketingyour.biz (Accessed 6 December 2018).

Bizzabo (2018). The Event Success Formula. Bizzabo. Available at: https://welcome.bizzabo.com/event-success-formula (Accessed 15 August 2018).

Bonnaud, S. (2016). Exhibiting in the US: A Short Guide for Foreign and European Companies. Available at: www.linkedin.com/pulse/exhibiting-us-short-guide-foreign-european-companies-sylvain-bonnaud (Accessed 15 August 2018).

Campanaro, T. (2017). Building a Successful Exhibit Staff (Why Your Booth Team Training Is So Important). GES. Available at: https://insights.ges.com/us-blog/building-a-successful-exhibit-staff-why-your-booth-team-training-is-so-important (Accessed 16 August 2018).

CiLT (2006). ELAN: Effects on the European Economy of Shortages of Foreign Language Skills in Enterprise. European Commission. Available at: http://ec.europa.eu/assets/eac/languages/policy/strategic-framework/documents/elan_en.pdf (Accessed 16 August 2018).

CompuSystems (2010). Your Exhibitor Success Kit. Available at: www.compusystems.com/images/eblast/ExhibitorSuccess.pdf" www.compusystems.com/images/eblast/ExhibitorSuccess.pdf (Accessed 14 January 2019).

CRE8AGENCY (2016). The Long-Term Impact of Trade Show Giveaways. CRE8AGENCY. Available at: http://cre8agency.com/the-long-term-impact-of-trade-show-giveaways (Accessed 16 August 2018).

Davis, J. (2014). The Most Overlooked Key to RSNA Exhibiting Success. The Radiological Society of North America. Available at: www.rsna.org/uploadedFiles/RSNA/Content/Annual_Meeting/Technical_Exhibits/1_OverlookedKey.pdf (Accessed 8 November 2018).

Davis, J. (2018). Preparing for Lead Follow-up Before the Show. Trade Shows. Available at: www.tradeshowturnaround.com/preparing-for-lead-follow-up-before-the-show (Accessed 15 August 2018).

Display Wizard (2018). 20 Trade Show Statistics That Will Blow Your Mind! Display Wizard. Available at: www.displaywizard.co.uk/20-amazing-trade-show-statistics (Accessed 14 August 2018).

Ellett, J. (2010). How long does it take your customer to form an opinion? Nfusion. Available at: http://nfusion.com/blog/how-long-does-it-take-your-customer-to-form-an-opinion (Accessed 16 August 2018).

Endless Events (2018). Event Marketing Stats. Endless Events. Available at: https://helloendless.com/event-marketing-stats (Accessed 16 August 2018).

Eventbrite (2018). An Introduction to Events. The UK Events Industry in Numbers. Available at: www.eventbrite.co.uk/blog/academy/uk-event-industry-in-numbers-ds00 (Accessed 14 August 2018).

Exhibitor Magazine (2018). Exhibitor Magazine's Economic Outlook Survey – Economic Outlook.Available at: www.exhibitoronline.com/topics/article.asp?ID=2541 (accessed 12 December 2018).

Gardiner, M. (2015). CEIR report reveals benchmarks for trade show evaluation. Exhibition World. Available at: www.exhibitionworld.co.uk/2015/07/28/ceir-report-reveals-benchmarks-for-trade-show-evaluation (Accessed 16 August 2018).

GraphiColor Exhibits (2017). Trade Show Statistics. Successful Exhibiting. Available at: https://graphicolor.com/blog/10-impressive-statistics-trade-show-marketing-program (Accessed 14 August 2018).

Hainla, L. (2018). 21 Social Media Marketing Statistics You Need to Know in 2018. Dreamgrow.com. Available at: www.dreamgrow.com/21-social-media-marketing-statistics (Accessed 14 August 2018).

Hughes, M (2007). The Value of Exhibiting in a Downturn. Tradeshow Week Magazine. Available at: https://archerytrade.org/wp-content/uploads/2018/01/exhibiting_downturn.pdf (Accessed 16 August 2018).

Ismail, N. (2017). Unsocial Media: A Tipping Point. Information Age. Available at: www.information-age.com/unsocial-media-tipping-point-123463994 (Accessed 15 August 2018).

Laja, P. (2018). First Impressions Matter: The Importance of Great Visual Design. CXL. Available at: https://conversionxl.com/blog/first-impressions-matter-the-importance-of-great-visual-design (Accessed 7 November 2018).

Levin, M. (2017). The 5 Most Important Trade Show Investments to Generate a Strong ROI. Inc.com. Available at: www.inc.com/marissa-levin/setting-your-2018-trade-show-budget-these-5-investments-will-make-your-time-money-worthwhile.html (Accessed 14 August 2018).

Lincoln West (2016). 10 Powerful Stats on the Value of Trade Shows. Available at: www.lincolnwest.co.uk/node/112 (Accessed 16 August 2018).

McAteer, O. (2018). Gen Z is Quitting Social Media in Droves Because It Makes Them Unhappy, Study Finds. Campaign US. Available at: www.campaignlive.com/article/gen-z-quitting-social-media-droves-makes-unhappy-study-finds/1459007 (Accessed 15 August 2018).

Marketing Charts (2013). 31% of Marketers Consider Events Essential to Doing Business. Marketing Charts. Available at: www.marketingcharts.com/cross-media-and-traditional/trade-shows-and-events-traditional-and-cross-channel-28915 (Accessed 14 August 2018).

Matthes, J. (2018). 20 Powerful Stats on the Value of Trade Shows and Expos. Spingo. Available at: www.spingo.com/blog/post/20-powerful-stats-on-the-value-of-trade-shows-and-expos (Accessed 15 August 2018).

Milloway, M. (2016). How Year-Round Social Media & Event Marketing Via Mobile Boosts Engagement. Apps for Events. Available at: www.appsforevents.com/news-blog/social-media-event-marketing-mobile-apps (Accessed 16 August 2018).

Russo, M. (2017). How to Powerup at Trade Shows (Infographic). Eprex Exhibition Displays. Available at: www.expressexhibitiondisplays.co.uk/event-marketing-tips/exhibiting-tips-infographic (Accessed 15 August 2018).

Sang, A. (2017). Event Marketing Budgets and Trends Statistics. Bizzabo. Available at: https://blog.bizzabo.com/event-marketing-statistics (Accessed 16 August 2018).

Schroeder, K. (2012). Getting the Most From Your Trade Show Experience. AAGD Pre-Trade Show Seminar. Available at: www.thevendorguide.com/aagdseminar2012.pdf (Accessed 7 November 2018).

Sikandar, M. (2018). 100 Social Media Statistics You Must Know. Statusbrew. Available at: https://blog.statusbrew.com/social-media-statistics-2018-for-business (Accessed 14 August 2018).

Statista (2018). E-commerce Worldwide. Statista. Available at: www.statista.com/topics/871/online-shopping (Accessed 15 August 2018).

Skyline (2008). International Exhibiting Trends & Outlook. Tradeshow Week Magazine. Available at: www.industrialcouncil.com/uploads/1/4/2/8/14286161/white_papers-intl_event_exhibitor-feb2008.final_2.pdf (Accessed 16 August 2018).

Skyline (2010). The Evolving Role of Exhibit Marketers. Tradeshow Week Magazine. Available at: www.skylinewhitespace.com/wp-content/uploads/2014/07/Evolving-Role-of-the-Exhibitor.pdf (Accessed 16 August 2018).

Skyline (2011). The Value of Trade Shows. EXPO Magazine. Available at: www.skylinewhitespace.com/wp-content/uploads/2014/07/The-Value-of-Exhibitions.pdf (Accessed 15 August 2018).

Stanton, T (2010). The Myths of Lead Management. Exhibitor Online. Available at: www.exhibitoronline.com/topics/article.asp?ID=742 (Accessed 16 August 2018).

Stanton, T. (2018). Economic Outlook. Exhibitor Online. Available at: www.exhibitoronline.com/topics/article.asp?ID=2541 (Accessed 15 August 2018).

Thimmesch, M. (2013). 16 Powerful Stats on the Value of Trade Shows. Skyline Exhibits. Available at: www.skyline.com/blog/posts/16-powerful-stats-on-the-value-of-trade-shows (Accessed 16 August 2018).

Tschabitscher, H. (2018). The Number of Emails Sent Per Day (and 20 Crazy Email Statistics). Available at: www.lifewire.com/how-many-emails-are-sent-every-day-1171210 (Accessed 15 August 2018).

UFI (2014). The Global Association of the Exhibition Industry. UFI. Available at: www.ufi.org/wp-content/uploads/2016/01/2014_exhibiton_industry_statistics_b.pdf (Accessed 14 August 2018).

UFI (2018). 20th UFI Global Exhibition Barometer. UFI. Available at: www.ufi.org/wp-content/uploads/2018/01/UFI_Global_Exhibition_Barometer_report20_b.pdf (Accessed 15 August 2018).

XL Displays (2017). Exhibition Statistics Exhibitors Should Keep in Mind. XL Displays. Available at: www.xldisplays.co.uk/news/186/Exhibition-Statistics-Exhibitors-Should-Keep-in-Mind.html (Accessed 16 August 2018).